The Little Book of Mindfulness

By Matt Valentine

Table of Contents

Wakefulness is the way to life.
The fool sleeps
As if he were already dead,
But the master is awake
And he lives forever.

He watches.
He is clear.

How happy he is!
For he sees that wakefulness is life.
How happy he is,
Following the path of the awakened.

– The Buddha

Introduction

It's difficult to fully capture the essence of mindfulness in words. On one end, you could describe it as a specific type of paying attention to the present moment. Sounds simple enough, but that definition doesn't describe the whole of what mindfulness is. On the other end, you could say mindfulness is like having an aura of light which emanates from you. A light which peels back the layers of your perception and allows you to experience reality in its true form, filled with absolute peace, joy, and true freedom. That one does a good job of describing the purpose of mindfulness, but even it doesn't fully capture the essence mindfulness completely. And if that second one sounded a bit deep, that's because it was. Mindfulness, along with its partner concentration, is the very act of looking and living deeply. Mindfulness is itself *the very energy of life itself.*

To be mindful is in fact to be truly alive. By truly alive, I mean a state in which you're completely and absolutely awake to this very moment of your life. Without mindfulness, we float through life only half awake, not fully aware of what's happening around or inside of us. This starves us of much of the joy in life. But I don't just mean that if you're walking down the street you won't notice the flowers in someone's garden as you pass by. I mean that even if you see a flower you won't really be able to see the *true flower*. The true flower is itself a flower. You can see, smell, and touch it. You know it's there and you know it's a flower. But at the same time the true flower isn't a flower at all. To see the true flower means to see that the flower is made up of all non-flower elements. The sun, the rain, the soil, the various elements in the soil, and the gardener who watered the flower. If you were to return even one of these elements to their source the flower would cease to exist. And the same can be said

1

of you. To see the true flower, and to know that you're intrinsically connected to it and everything else around you, is to experience a deep sense of peace and joy. This is what it means to live deeply with mindfulness. By living deeply with mindfulness we can touch the ground of our being. But this isn't some esoteric philosophical concept. There's no intellectual explanations, no theories, and no guesswork with mindfulness. Mindfulness isn't about beliefs. *It's about what is.* It's about discovering your true nature. By living deeply *in this moment* you can touch the ground of your being and experience true peace and happiness.

I was first introduced to mindfulness through a book. It was a beautiful book and I learned so much about mindfulness from it that still to this day I come back to learn from it. But it never provided an adequate enough explanation of what mindfulness was. In fact, nothing really captured the full extent of the power and practice of mindfulness. It's because of this that I wasted a lot of time in the beginning stages of my own mindfulness practice. I absorbed as much information as possible, practiced to the best of my ability, and still didn't seem to get things right. It took some time before I really understood what mindfulness was and how to practice it correctly. It's because of both the incredible impact that mindfulness has had on my own life and because of what I went through to properly learn mindfulness that I felt compelled to write about what I had learned and provide a resource that others could use that would make learning about and adopting the practice of mindfulness clear and straightforward.

The Little Book of Mindfulness is about teaching you what mindfulness is, why mindfulness is important, how to practice mindfulness, and how to develop mindfulness as a habit in simple and clear language. Mindfulness has been practiced for some 2,500 years by the Buddha and his long lineage of disciples, as well as many other spiritual traditions (whether they call it mindfulness or not). It isn't the only key to spiritual awakening or even just a healthy personal practice. But it is one of, if not the, most important pieces of a nourishing and healing spiritual practice which leads to true peace and happiness. I hope to present this great gift, a gift which was given to me in much the same manner, in the best way possible. To receive the gift of mindfulness is to receive the key which can change your entire life. I hope you'll accept this gift. In reality, it's not mine to give. It's already yours. You've had it all your life and you just didn't know it. Realize the incredible gift that this moment is.

How to Use *The Little Book of Mindfulness*

My primary goal in writing *The Little Book of Mindfulness* was to provide a convenient resource which broke down mindfulness in a way that made it crystal clear to understand, super easy to learn, and straightforward to apply as a new positive habit for anyone whether that person had prior knowledge or experience with mindfulness or not. *The Little Book of Mindfulness* is separated based on the three major aspects of adopting mindfulness as a daily practice: learning what mindfulness is, learning how to practice mindfulness, and learning how to bring mindfulness into your everyday life as a daily practice which nourishes your mind and body. Part 1 is titled *What is Mindfulness?* It covers, you guessed it, what mindfulness is along with a thorough explanation of its inner workings and the major benefits or reasons why someone should make mindfulness a part of their lives. Part 2 is titled *Practicing Mindfulness* and it covers the major mindfulness practices such as mindful sitting, mindful walking, mindful breathing, as well as a chapter on a number of common areas where the average person can practice mindfulness. Part 3 is titled *Developing Mindfulness* and it's all about developing mindfulness as a daily practice. This section is very important. Without Part 3 it would be easy to finish the book and then throw it to the wayside. The purpose of this book isn't to provide a bunch of information and then let you loose without any direction or guidance. If you follow the suggestions in Part 3 you'll have a whole array of techniques which you can use to immediately begin applying mindfulness as a part of your daily life.

And so it's for this reason that I felt a simple introduction wouldn't suffice. This short section is about how to make the most of *The Little Book of Mindfulness*. So there's a few key points that I'd like to cover. Below is a small list of points you should keep in mind when reading. By keeping these points in mind you'll enhance your reading experience and make the most of the information provided. Don't just read this book and think you'll know how to practice mindfulness all of a sudden. It takes actual practice and some patience. But by following the tips that follow you'll ensure you cultivate an environment conducive to developing mindfulness.

1. Read *with mindfulness*

I want you to strive to read as much of this book *in mindfulness* as possible. Let this book be not just a book, but a place to begin developing your practice of mindfulness. Let it also be a lesson that you can practice mindfulness anywhere and at any time. That is, if you remember, which can be difficult with how much the average person keeps on their plate. But I'm getting ahead of myself, we'll have a chapter for tackling that later. Now, you might be thinking, "But I don't know how to practice mindfulness, how am I supposed to read this book in mindfulness?" Don't worry, we'll go over that in the next chapter. So for now, you'll have to wait. Keep these tips in mind though: In order to read this book in mindfulness, particularly if you're just beginning your practice, you'll want to minimize distractions before you read. This includes distractions from within. Empty your mind (as much as possible) before reading. If there's something you're worried about or are having a hard time getting out of your head, imagine yourself gently placing it aside and tell yourself it's OK to bring it back once you're done reading. Put 100% of your focus onto reading the book. Read the book with all of your being. During this time, as with anytime you practice mindfulness, nothing else matters more than what you're doing in that moment. In this case, nothing matters more than the act of reading. Be fully present for every single word. If your thoughts stray, acknowledge the thought and come back to the book. By reading the book in this way you open your mind fully to the information in this book. This can do a number of beautiful things, such as improve your ability to absorb the content and make reading more enjoyable. Not to mention, you begin practicing mindfulness for yourself. Don't worry about knowing everything about mindfulness right now, what's important is that you make the effort.

2. Take your time

Take your time and really enjoy every page with all of your being. This book isn't meant to be raced through. To increase your chances of absorbing the information and really using it to apply positive change to your life you need to take your time and let certain pieces of information "sit" in your consciousness so to speak. After reading the chapter on "Awakening to Your True Nature", for instance, you might want to take a day off and contemplate on the material. At this point, you'll have been introduced to mindfulness and know what it's all about so you should be able to also start practicing mindfulness in your everyday life in between reading sessions.

And if you're thinking it might take a while to read this entire book in mindfulness, erase such thoughts right now. Reading is a chance to learn something new which can positively affect your life, don't pass up that chance by trying to rush through the book just for the satisfaction of being able to tell yourself "I read a new book!" Really take your time and absorb the information presented. Mindfulness can completely change your life. Don't pass up the opportunity.

3. Take action

If you want to really take everything you can from reading *The Little Book of Mindfulness*, you can't just read the book. Reading the book itself in mindfulness is a great start, but you also need to put what's talked about throughout the book into practice in your daily life. You need to take action.

Mindfulness works like anything else in life. That is, it's an action which has a certain amount of "energy" associated with it. This energy is all around us and in everything. And it pulls us in the direction we're accustomed to moving in unless we make it a point to redirect this energy. I'll explain this energy in more detail later, for now just know that it takes work to develop mindfulness as a regular part of your life. But it's infinitely worthwhile to do so, as I'll explain in Part 1. Be patient and don't expect to get it right from the start. Make it a point to be non-judgmental about your practice. That is, be aware of how you're behaving and what's occurring within your practice. But, don't judge yourself negatively no matter what happens. Go an entire day and forget to practice? That's OK, I had many days like that at the beginning. You'll get through it. Don't judge yourself or get discouraged, just keep moving forward one step at a time. I didn't have anyone to talk to on a daily basis or anyone teaching me personally in a monastery. I had to develop the habit essentially on my own. In Part 3 I'll show you the techniques which I used to establish the practice of mindfulness in my daily life.

You're now ready to venture into the world of mindfulness and discover what it means to be truly alive. I wanted to end by taking a second to say thanks for reading. I put my all into writing *The Little Book of Mindfulness,* so it's filled to the brim with valuable information. I originally planned for this book to be somewhere around fifty pages. But the "little" book of mindfulness turned out to be a bit larger than I originally thought (roughly double that, as you'll see). It's filled with valuable information, the same information that transformed my life in so many ways. If it in some way brings some sort of positive change to your own life then I'd love to hear from you (we'll connect again at the end of the book, where I'll show you how).

Peace,
Matt

Part 1:
What is Mindfulness?

The Origins of Mindfulness

~~~

The Buddha, also sometimes referred to as Shakyamuni or Guatama Buddha, was born Siddhārtha Gautama. Siddhārtha was born and lived some 2,400-2,600 years ago, likely between 500 and 400 BCE, in either what is now modern day India or Nepal. At the age of 29, Siddhārtha set out on a spiritual journey. He wanted to find a way to alleviate his suffering as well as the suffering of others. And ultimately, to find the true path to peace and happiness. Six years later, at the age of 35, Siddhārtha is said to have sat at the foot of the now famous Bodhi tree and achieved complete awakening (or enlightenment, in many English translations). For forty five years after his great awakening, Siddhārtha Gautama, now the Buddha, travelled around ancient India and Nepal spreading his teachings. And among those teachings was mindfulness.

When the Buddha was asked, "Sir, what do you and your monks practice?" he responded with, "We sit, we walk, and we eat." The man then asked, "But sir, everyone sits, walks, and eats." The Buddha replied, "When we sit, *we know* we are sitting. When we walk, *we know* we are walking. When we eat, *we know* we are eating." This was the Buddha's practice. But what exactly did he mean? The Buddha was referring to living fully in the present moment with *mindfulness*. Living in a way that we're fully awake to the present moment. To the Buddha, mindfulness was a matter of life or death. But not life or death in a literal sense. Rather, to do something in mindfulness is to become truly alive in that moment. The Buddha didn't discover mindfulness, he simply showed us how to use it to its full potential. Like a great lighthouse which illuminates the dark ocean, the Buddha showed us how to shine mindfulness like a light on ourselves and the world around us in order to unveil and break down the many roadblocks between us and true peace and happiness.

Mindfulness is often described in the West as, "having origins in ancient meditative practices" or something to that degree, and that a non-secular version of mindfulness has been adapted for professional use. There's nothing necessarily wrong with saying the origins of mindfulness are in ancient meditative or spiritual practices. This is a true statement. But by not *fully* recognizing or understanding where mindfulness came from it will be very difficult, if not impossible, to realize its full potential. Also, mindfulness is often misunderstood by some in the West as having an updated or modernized version of itself. But nothing, nor anyone, has ever changed what mindfulness is or how it functions. This misunderstanding likely stems from the West's general misunderstanding of the dharmic traditions as a whole. By dharmic I mean all those spiritual traditions which arose in and around ancient India- Buddhism, Hinduism, Yoga, and the lesser known Jainism. Mindfulness isn't inherently eastern, western, Buddhist, religious, or anything else. Mindfulness has no labels. Even "mindfulness" is just the word we use to describe it, it isn't mindfulness at all. Mindfulness is beyond language. It's a powerful and unchanging ability which we all possess the potential to express. Understanding this is important. But it's equally important to understand the origins of mindfulness in our world. When was it first used? Why was it used? How has that evolved?

Mindfulness is the English translation of the Sanskrit word "smrti" ("sati" in Pali) which translates literally as "memory". Brahmans of the Vedic faith in ancient India are thought to have used this complete presence of mind to recall huge bodies of text due to the fact that nothing was written down at the time. The Vedic faith, a precursor to modern Hinduism, is believed to have existed from 1750 to 500 B.C.E., which places its end point (500 B.C.E.) somewhere in or around the Buddha's life. But that wasn't all the Buddha adopted from the ancient Brahman tradition. "The four immeasurable minds" of love, compassion, equanimity, and joy are considered by many to be one of the highest teachings of Buddhism, which the Buddha adopted from the Vedic spiritual tradition. The Buddha was something of a scientist. Through diligent practice he saw the glimmers of truth that existed in each spiritual tradition of his time and sifted those truths out to form what would later be called Buddhism. This was based strictly on direct experience, as opposed to mere belief or superstition. It's probably for this very reason that the Buddha is said to have been able to speak skillfully to people from the language of their own tradition.

The Buddha adopted mindfulness in his own practice and

teaching, and used it to refer to both "memory" as well as "presence of mind". This was the birth of the mindfulness we know today. All of Buddhist scripture refers to mindfulness in this way.

Like a great lighthouse which illuminates the dark ocean, the Buddha showed us how to shine mindfulness like a light on ourselves and the world around us in order to unveil and break down the many roadblocks between us and true peace and happiness.

West Meets East

Fast-forward some 2,500 years and you arrive at the modern mindfulness "movement" in the West. Mindfulness began spreading throughout the United States about a quarter century ago, but it wasn't until the last decade that it really started picking up steam. And now, as of writing this, it's exploded in popularity all across the United States. Mindfulness has now expanded to Wall Street, Silicon Valley, major medical centers, hospitals, countless companies, and even many classrooms throughout the United States. Entire magazines, blogs, and of course, books, devoted to mindfulness have arisen from this as well. And it continues to spread by the day. If you had to pinpoint what caused mindfulness to spread throughout the West in recent decades, it would be because of Thich Nhat Hanh, Jon Kabat-Zinn, and the scientific research on mindfulness.

It all started with a Vietnamese Zen master, writer, and peace activist by the name of Thich Nhat Hanh. Thich Nhat Hanh has traveled the world, including the US, for decades spreading Buddhist wisdom, such as mindfulness, and advocating peace. After many years of experience with mindfulness and meditation as well as participating in retreats led by Thich Nhat Hanh, Jon Kabat-Zinn, an American doctor, created the Mindfulness Based Stress Reduction program (MBSR), an eight-week course meant to treat a wide range of conditions (particularly stress) through the use of mindfulness. That was in 1979, and since then the MBSR program has spread throughout the United States and made mindfulness the target of literally hundreds of scientific studies.

But it's the exceptional results of these scientific studies that are what have really convinced so many professional institutions to adopt the practice of mindfulness. In the modern world, when science gets behind something, people take notice. And that's just what happened. After the first few studies were released mindfulness began spreading like wildfire. The only criticism that's been given of this movement is in the fact that many are adopting mindfulness as a way to become more productive and efficient at their jobs as opposed to the original purpose of mindfulness as a tool for discovering one's true nature and becoming happy and at peace. This is undoubtedly misguided, but something I see us becoming conscious, or mindful, of in the near future. This is only the beginning of a more conscious existence for the world at large. There's no telling just how far and wide mindfulness and the realization of the importance of living more consciously will spread. The reason it's being adopted by certain people and institutions may not be completely pure. But one thing is for certain: by living with mindfulness we'll be guided towards a happier, more peaceful, and overall better existence for ourselves and for those around us. It just might take us a while to realize that this is really what we're searching for.

Mindfulness is...

What exactly *is* mindfulness? In a nutshell, mindfulness can be defined as ***the complete and nonjudgmental aware-ness of the present moment.*** It's also been defined as "the moment to moment awareness of present events". In fact, it's been defined dozens, if not hundreds, of times and most of those definitions suffice. There's no one agreed upon way of defining mindfulness. This is because mindfulness is a state of being be-yond words or concepts. One must practice mindfulness in or-der to truly understand what mindfulness is. As I mentioned in the last chapter, the origin of the word mindfulness is in the Pali word "sati", and its Sanskrit counterpart "smrti", which both lit-erally mean "memory". But perhaps more precisely they repre-sent "presence of mind" or "attentiveness to the present". This is what the Buddha was referring to when he said, "When we sit, *we know* we are sitting. When we walk, *we know* we are walk-ing. When we eat, *we know* we are eating." He meant that when he and his disciples sat, walked, or ate they were fully present for the act of sitting, walking, or eating.

Even when becoming lost in thought, while practicing mind-fulness the practitioner is fully aware that they just became lost in a particular thought and are mindful of the thought itself. This is because mindfulness isn't just mindfulness of an object in the present moment such as one's breath, steps, or food. It's also mindfulness of anything which might arise in the present moment while concentrating on an object. In a way, mindful-ness is the *observer of change*. While concentrating on the ob-ject of meditation, such as one's breath or steps, we become distracted by thoughts, feelings, and other sensations. These are "changes" in the field of mindfulness, the area which mind-fulness observes. In this way think of mindfulness as a motion detector. If nothing moves, if nothing changes, then nothing is detected. Mindfulness is still there observing, just as the motion detector which detects no motion is still there observing its area of detection, but until a thought, feeling, or some other sensation arises the practitioner just continues to concentrate on the object of meditation. When this happens is when the real work begins.

Mindfulness is the complete and nonjudgmental awareness of the present moment.

Think of mindfulness as a "field of attention" with a point of concentration in the center acting as an anchor to the present, rather than just a pointed concentration on something while pushing away everything else around you. Imagine a dream catcher. The idea behind a dream catcher is it's supposed to "catch" your bad dreams as you're sleeping. Just as a dream catcher catches your bad dreams, imagine each thought, feeling, and sensation being caught by your "field of mindfulness". Except in this case, you don't label any thought, feeling, or sensation either good or bad. While in mindfulness, each thought, feeling, and sensation that arises automatically enters into this field of mindfulness and, this is the important part, is gently acknowledged and accepted "as it is". By "as it is" I mean without judging it in any way. If this is hard to imagine, don't worry. For the most part this nonjudgmental awareness happens naturally when you practice mindfulness correctly. The important thing to remember for now is that mindfulness is not a rejection of anything. Mindfulness is an open acceptance of everything that comes into your awareness. If you're practicing mindful breathing, don't reject thoughts that come into your mind just because they interrupt your mindful breathing. Observing these thoughts, which are typically unnoticed but always dispersing our awareness and coloring our perception, is a major part of practicing mindfulness. So this is perfectly fine. Simply acknowledge the thought in mindfulness, just as you were doing with your breath, and then let the thought pass. Then bring your focus *back to your breath*. As time goes on your ability to concentrate on one point for a period of time as well as your ability to detect things with your mindfulness will improve. And with it, the quality of your mindfulness practice will improve as well.

Mindfulness has a number of different "qualities". If you break mindfulness down based on these qualities it becomes much easier to understand it as a whole. We've covered the basic workings of mindfulness so far, but in order to gain a deeper understanding of mindfulness let's break it down and look at each quality individually. There's 6 key aspects of mindfulness which I'll cover below.

Mindfulness is...

1. Mindfulness *of something*

Mindfulness is always mindfulness *of something*. It's not just a conscious directing of your awareness to the present moment, it's a conscious directing of your awareness to *something* which is occurring or existing in the present moment. Common centers of focus are your breath, steps, or some other area or areas of the body. Concentration, or samadhi in Sanskrit, is a force which works in tandem with mindfulness. Concentration is "single-pointedness of mind" and it's just that- the act of focusing on a single point.

While practicing mindfulness you will be developing your power of concentration as well as your mindfulness. There is no separating mindfulness and concentration. They're partners on the path to attaining a tranquil and clear mind. Think of concentration as the "hard" force and mindfulness as the "soft". Concentration is exactly what it sounds like, it's the forceful act of focusing on a single point. Imagine your field of mindfulness enveloping everything within your perception in a soft glow. Next, imagine a thin line piercing out from your mindfulness directly to an object. This is your concentration. Mindfulness, on the other hand, is a sort of soft awareness. Remember the dream catcher? Mindfulness is the field of awareness which then "sees" everything that arises while concentrating on an object. Mindfulness is what notices when your concentration lapses and your thoughts stray. Think of mindfulness as the ultimate, voiceless, and nonjudgmental observer. It judges nothing. It makes no distinctions. It simply observes everything that comes into its field of awareness. Your concentration, the force anchoring your mindfulness to some object in the present moment (the object of meditation), is the instrument of mindfulness. Mindfulness decides where the point of concentration will be. It observes the anchor point (the point of your concentration), notices when concentration strays, and where it strays to. This might be difficult to imagine at first, but for now just know that the act of practicing mindfulness will feel much like concentrating on an object, such as your breathing, and then doing your best to notice or acknowledge when your thoughts stray. Just being able to acknowledge when your thoughts stray will take some time. In the beginning, your practice will look and feel like this: 1) concentrate on your breath, 2) lose concentration, sometimes aware of the thought or feeling you strayed to, most of the time not, 3) back to concentrating on your breathing. That's it. But after a while you'll begin to notice these thoughts and feelings more often, more clearly, and that will allow you to acknowledge them with your mindfulness.

2. Mindfulness of something *in the present moment*

Moving on from the last point, mindfulness is always mindfulness of something *in the present moment*. But it doesn't have to be something existing in the physical world. As we spoke about earlier, that can be mindfulness of a thought that arises in the present moment while concentrating on your breath, body, or some other object. What mindfulness *isn't* is reflecting on the past or thinking about the future. When reflecting on the past or thinking about the future you're consciously directing your attention to the past, future, or some altogether imagined place. Therefore it's not something which exists in the present moment. Mindfulness is always the observing of what is occurring *in the present moment*.

As we go about our daily lives, we often don't notice how our perception, or mental filters, such as bias affect how we see the world around us. And we think that what we're thinking and seeing with our eyes are two different things. But they aren't. What we see with our eyes passes through our perception before we even realize we see the object. It's like we have an internal check point which we've built up from our life experiences. And this check point has, over the years, gotten filled with both good and bad things which "color" our perception and affect our experiences. In this way, you and your mindfulness are like the house cleaners come to clean up this internal check point and empty it of all those things keeping you from experiencing reality in its true form. Imagine someone offers you a piece of food which you've never tried before. This food somewhat resembles, say, Brussels sprouts (bleh!). As soon as you lay eyes on it you have a negative sensation. Maybe you get a bad taste in your mouth, your body cringes a little, and a bad memory of eating Brussels sprouts flashes into your mind. This new food item could be amazing. You have no idea if it is or isn't. You've never actually tried it. But your perception has already completely colored your experience to the point where it can even affect how it will taste. This is an example of how our perception colors everything around us. Everything you perceive *is your mind*. You might think you're observing your breath, a Brussels sprout, or a flower. But what you're really observing is *your perception* of those things. Mindfulness is about observing what is occurring in the present moment so that you can pierce through your wrong perceptions to witness reality as it is without any mental filters getting in the way. This is why mindfulness is mindfulness of something in the present moment. The point of mindfulness is to experience reality as it is, allowing you to touch the true peace and joy of each moment.

3. A *conscious decision*

Mindfulness is a purposeful directing of your consciousness to the present, it doesn't happen on accident. To be fully awake to the present moment you have to decide "I am fully awake to this moment" by directing your consciousness to an object in the present moment. You decide to be mindful in any given moment. It doesn't happen by accident.

I mentioned earlier how the point of your concentration, or object of meditation, works as your anchor point to the present moment. The starting point for the anchor and the eventual anchor point is this conscious decision. Think of mindfulness as a ship and you're the captain. You make the conscious decision to place the anchor down and where to place it. You then throw the anchor, your concentration, off the ship. The anchor then hits the intended anchor point, or object of meditation, where it will rest. Of course at first this anchor won't be very strong. It will be made of, say, plastic. Not a very good anchor. But with time it will develop into a heavy and resilient anchor.

4. *Nonjudgmental* awareness

All spiritual practice in an overall sense is about finding true peace and happiness through accomplishing total liberation (or freedom) from the various factors that hold us back. And so we become liberated by discovering the truth. That is, by uncovering all those things which cloud our vision. *This is the ultimate purpose of mindfulness.* It's this nonjudgmental awareness that makes mindfulness so important in finding true peace and happiness.

Mindfulness accepts everything as it is. As I mentioned earlier it makes no distinctions, holds no bias, and is completely separated from all mental filters which distort your perception of reality. Mindfulness allows you to experience true reality. This is liberation. And as I also mentioned earlier, if you're not sure how to do this at first then don't worry. Mindfulness is itself nonjudgmental. It's helpful to keep this point in mind at times, but you'll find this will happen somewhat naturally. If you sense bias or get the feeling that you're somehow coloring your perception of something while practicing then this is a good thing. Simply by noticing this it means you're becoming mindful of your various mental filters. If this happens, know that you're on the right path. As always, simply acknowledge it and bring yourself back to your object of meditation. It's not wrong that you lose your concentration. What's wrong is not observing the distraction with mindfulness.

5. Developed *like a muscle*

Mindfulness works like a muscle. At the beginning your energy of mindfulness will be very weak. But over time your mindfulness will strengthen and you'll notice a significant difference both in your ability to concentrate and in your ability to see with mindfulness. This is important to know at the beginning because it's at the very beginning stages where things are most difficult. While trying to establish the practice of mindfulness as a part of your life you'll be constantly fighting old habits. In Buddhism, this is sometimes called "habit energy". Imagine everything you do carries with it a certain energy. The more you do something the more energy it develops, and with it, the more "pull" it has.

You can develop energy anywhere in your life, in both positive and negative places. So when starting out don't become discouraged when you're having a hard time sticking to your mindfulness practice, such as when you forget to practice for an entire day altogether. I went through this constantly at first and it's just going to be a battle. There's no two ways about it. Part 3 is all about helping you develop mindfulness in your daily life and it includes some great tips and tricks, all of which I've used to develop my own mindfulness practice.

6. Like turning on the "HD" switch to your life

Most of the time, without us even knowing it, our consciousness is split in many directions. It's split between various sensations in the present moment and various thoughts in our mind. When sitting at your computer at work, for instance, you could be typing up an email, but really, you're typing up the email while semi-listening to two people talk a few feet away from you, noticing how cold you are, thinking about that episode of Lost you watched last night, and thinking about the fact that you feel like you're gaining some weight. That's really what the "present moment" looks and feels like for most of us: our consciousness, bouncing constantly from one place to another. As you begin practicing mindfulness, you'll start to observe this very behavior for yourself. This bouncing around makes us live in a way to where we're only half-awake to anything that occurs around us. Let's call this life in "standard-definition". More on this in a bit.

The last point I'd like to cover in this chapter is that it's important for you to know what mindfulness *feels* like. I can put as many words as I'd like on a page describing how it works, how to do it, the benefits of doing it, and you could read it all, but if I don't clearly explain how you'll feel while truly being mindful then you won't have much more than a guess at whether or not you're really practicing mindfulness properly or not. So what does mindfulness *feel* like? In a few words...it feels like turning on the "HD" (High-Definition) switch to your life. By that I mean that the moment you make the conscious decision "I'm now fully aware of what I'm doing and what's happening to me in the present moment" you should feel as though you've come alive. As though, before you made that conscious decision and "activated" your mindfulness, you were half-asleep. You'll notice things you never noticed before and everything around you will be magnified.

Don't expect the feeling to be that intense at first though. When you first start practicing the feeling will be subtle, which is all the more reason why one of the first mindfulness practices you adopt should be mindful sitting (traditionally just called sitting meditation, which we'll cover in Part 2). While sitting quietly in mindfulness you'll make the greatest progress towards improving your concentration and developing your mindfulness, as opposed to doing a more difficult activity before you've really developed your skill level. This is because you'll have fewer distractions and will be able to "hone in" on the feeling I described in the last chapter better. Once you've developed your mindfulness though it will be highly beneficial to practice mindfulness of more difficult tasks in order to develop your skill.

One last note. Even if you're just beginning with mindfulness, while you might not be able to tell exactly what thoughts arise in your mind, you should still begin noticing these distractions as they arise. Simply noticing that some sort of distraction just arose in your mind is the second feeling you should look out for, even if at first you don't know what the thoughts or feelings are exactly. Take these two feelings described together and you'll have a much clearer picture of what mindfulness should feel like. Use the information I described in this point to guide your practice in the beginning.

Breaking down mindfulness into parts helps us understand how it works. But we need to make sure not to make the mistake of actually thinking of mindfulness as a bunch of separate things. Mindfulness is one thing: ***a complete and nonjudgmental awareness of the present moment.*** It's the conscious act of bringing one's complete awareness into the present reality, which allows us to see the world in a way we've never seen it before- beyond our wrong perceptions (and perception itself), preconceived notions, deep-seated emotions, and beyond the ego. Seeing reality in its purest state, filled with a limitless peace, joy, and freedom.

The moment you make the conscious decision "I am going to be fully aware of what I'm doing here and what's happening to me in the present moment" you should feel as though you've come alive. As though, before you made that conscious decision and "activated" your mindfulness, you were half-asleep.

Mindfulness isn't...

We live in an age where communication is instantaneous, whether across the globe or right next door, and just about anyone with an internet connection can access a limitless amount of information on any subject that's ever existed. It's a beautiful and interesting time to be alive. We have the ability to do so many positive things with this new connected world. But it's also because of this, combined with mindfulness' quick adoption in the West, that quite a few misconceptions about what mindfulness is have cropped up. People have begun jumping on mindfulness like a bandwagon, using it as a tool for nothing more than increased productivity and a little stress reduction. This is greatly limiting its full capability. On top of this, or perhaps because of this, many incorrect or dubious explanations of *how* to practice mindfulness have cropped up as well.

But there's more to it than just that. Mindfulness itself can be confusing if not explained clearly and thoroughly (and ultimately, experienced personally). To the beginner it can sound like a simple paying attention to something in the present moment. And that is, in large part, what mindfulness is. But there's more to it. And if what it is and how to practice it isn't clearly explained then you can end up wasting an inordinate amount of time in the beginning. Visual examples, like the ship, the ship's captain and the anchor example in the previous chapter, can really help one get a basic understanding. But actual practice also needs to be stressed. Mindfulness isn't a blog post, it's an activity.

In this chapter, I hope to clear up a few important misconceptions about mindfulness as a whole in order to save you time and improve the quality of your mindfulness practice right from the get-go. Here I'll be covering more than just things that have to do with exact functions of mindfulness, as opposed to the last chapter, I'll also be covering common misconceptions about mindfulness as I mentioned above.

Mindfulness isn't...

1. **A tool for productivity**

This is a major mistake of the West's adoption of mindfulness. There isn't anything necessarily wrong with using mindfulness in order to be more effective or productive. But the purpose of the West's mass adoption of mindfulness has been almost exclusively as a tool for increased productivity and effectiveness. This isn't good. It's being used towards our obsession over productivity, which itself is misguided. Sure, if everyone starts becoming mindful all day long in order to be more productive it's not the worst thing in the world. But adopting mindfulness to serve our obsession with productivity would be a grave misuse of this powerful tool which can completely change one's life. Mindfulness is to be used to improve your well-being, not feed your ego. It can calm and quiet the restless mind, help one obtain complete rest, uncover deep-seated negative emotions and limiting beliefs and help heal them, erase wrong perceptions in order to bring a greater sense of peace and happiness to ourselves and those around us, and ultimately, to take us beyond all perception to experience our true nature. In the West we need to discover the practice of "right mindfulness". If we can do this, we can make great use of the growing exposure of this amazing spiritual tool.

2. Only a form of sitting meditation

In the West, mindfulness is often misunderstood by some as simply a form of sitting meditation and nothing else. When someone says they practice mindfulness they likely only practice it for 15-20 minutes in the morning once a day in the form of mindful sitting (also called sitting meditation). This is great. Better than not doing any meditation at all. But mindfulness is far more than just a form of sitting meditation. It's a meditation technique which can and should be used throughout the day. You should strive to live each waking moment in mindfulness. As I spoke about earlier, mindfulness is like life in HD. You know that feeling when you look at a standard definition television and then immediately look over at a high definition one? Mindfulness is like that. You see a whole slew of things throughout your day that you never noticed before. I don't necessarily mean you notice beautiful scenery more often though, although this does happen, I mean that when you turn your mindfulness "switch" on you immediately feel different. You feel completely....alive. There's really no other way to describe it. Don't starve your spiritual or personal practice by simply using mindfulness as a form of sitting meditation. Discover the true power and beauty of mindfulness by using it during your everyday life.

3. Simply paying close attention or strongly focusing

It's difficult at first to fully grasp what mindfulness is. At first it will probably be difficult to understand just how it differs from simple paying close attention to or strongly focusing on something. This is a natural misunderstanding. Remember, mindfulness is like a soft focus. It's the quiet observer which sits atop one's concentration observing everything. Concentration is what creates the vantage point for mindfulness. Without it, there is no point with which to reliably observe reality.

4. Difficult

By this I mean two things: mindfulness isn't difficult to learn and mindfulness isn't difficult to practice. First, the act of being mindful shouldn't feel like you're straining your eyeballs. You shouldn't feel like you're going to give yourself a headache. The soft focus example doesn't just serve to explain the function of mindfulness, it also explains the feeling of being mindful. Mindfulness feels like a soft focus as opposed to a hard one that hurts your head. You should feel absolutely no strain in your head, cringing in your face, or tension in your mind. Mindfulness should feel effortless and be enjoyable. You should look forward to practicing mindfulness because you know you'll feel truly alive when doing so.

Secondly, it's not difficult to learn mindfulness. There's just a lot of bad explanations on how to practice it (whether intentional or not). And to some extent, you just have to get out there and practice in order to learn. Nowadays, if you type "mindfulness" into Google you'll get literally millions of results. Everyone's talking about it and, you guessed it, everyone thinks they know what it is and how to teach it with little experience. Again, it doesn't take an expert to be able to understand and explain mindfulness clearly. But many people are just trying to use the popularity of mindfulness to attract readers or viewers and in reality know very little about it. Use careful scrutiny in deciding who to listen to for advice on developing your mindfulness practice. You'll hear me say this a few times. That's because it's so important.

5. Religious

I've seen a lot of particularly academic sources explaining mindfulness in a way that it was once a technique attached to a religion or a system of philosophy (Buddhism), but that scientists have now adapted a "non-secular" version of it. Don't let this confuse you. Mindfulness is mindfulness. No one can make it religious or non-religious or anything else. And anyone who describes mindfulness in this way has a very limited understanding of its purpose as well as its origin.

Buddhism in and of itself is about discovering the truth of this world, including yourself, through your own direct experience. The Buddha taught his disciples not to follow his teachings on blind faith. He insisted they closely examine and scrutinize everything, even his own teachings, in order to discover their validity. And with it, the truth. And to that end *mindfulness is one's master tool*. It allows the practitioner to shine a "light" so to speak on their lives in order to discover the true nature of themselves and the world around them. It's like a scientist using a magnifying glass to view a sample. The scientist views that sample in order to find something which hasn't yet been noticed and to ultimately gain a better understanding of what's being viewed and eventually contribute to improving life in some way with this knowledge. Mindfulness is your magnifying glass. It allows you to see things you wouldn't otherwise be able to see without it and ultimately gain a better understanding of everything around you. Specifically, from the vantage point of yourself. The wise, including the Buddha, long ago learned that if you work to understand the self you inadvertently gain a deeper understanding of the world around you. Buddhists practice mindfulness. But Buddhism is simply the practice of discovering and living true peace and happiness. And mindfulness itself is simply the practice of being truly alive. Understand that when you practice mindfulness, *you practice the art of living deeply as a living being*. Nothing more is necessary. This can be called Buddhism and it can be called striving to live life fully in the peace of the present moment. They're one in the same.

6. Only for certain people

Mindfulness isn't something that works for some people and doesn't for others. Don't look at mindfulness as an activity like dancing, sports, drawing, or the like. Think of it as a fundamental activity used to nourish the mind and body like eating, drinking, exercising, and sleeping. Mindfulness is a universal technique that anyone and everyone can use to improve the quality of their lives. Don't limit yourself by holding on to the wrong view that spiritual practice, in this case mindfulness, is only for certain people. It doesn't matter whether you really love practicing mindful walking, mindful drawing, or rather do something else in mindfulness altogether, the practice of mindfulness is for everyone. Children and adults, doctors and lawyers, teachers and business men or women, fathers and mothers, and everyone in between.

I bring this up because I've seen this reason used many times as an excuse for not pushing through the initial difficulty of learning to do something, including mindfulness. We often give up too soon after trying something new and convince ourselves either that we're just not good at it or that it "isn't for us". You wouldn't say that sleeping isn't for you, right? Think of mindfulness and meditation in the same way. Think of it as a necessary component for nourishing the mind and body that's available to everyone.

7. Something you do sometimes

Mindfulness isn't something you do sometimes. It isn't something you do only when you're feeling particularly stressed or anxious. There's a growing misconception that mindfulness is simply a tool for reducing stress. Stress is a real problem in today's world. Mindfulness' ability to not just reduce but completely remove stress altogether is of great benefit to a lot of people especially in fast-paced professional environments. This is really amazing. But to use mindfulness solely as a tool that's to be used sometimes when you're feeling stressed is another great misuse of this incredible tool.

At first, it will be extremely difficult to do more than meditate once or twice a day and maybe practice some mindful breathing every few hours for a minute or two. But after a while though, with the right energy put into your practice, you'll develop the ability to be mindful far more often. During basic activities like walking to and from your car at work, sweeping the floor, doing the dishes, and even driving. It's possible to be mindful every waking hour, and this is exactly what you should strive for.

And don't think you have to do things slower while in mindfulness. This is another common misconception. Once you've developed your ability you don't have to do things any slower than you usually would without mindfulness, so with practice it's very possible to be mindful all day long and get the same amount done (but in reality, you'll be *more* productive). If you strive to be mindful *throughout* each day you'll obtain the greatest benefits by far.

When you practice mindfulness, you practice the art of living deeply as a living being.

Finding Peace Within

So, now you have a general understanding of what mindfulness is. But why practice mindfulness? What's so important about being mindful? Knowing how mindfulness works is only part of what constitutes a complete understanding of mindfulness. In the last few chapters, I covered briefly some of the reasons why you should practice mindfulness. In this chapter, I'll expand on what I mentioned there and show you why mindfulness is the key to finding true peace and happiness.

All spiritual practice can be broken down into obtaining and maintaining two states: 1) a calm mind, and 2) a clear mind. In Buddhism, these two states are generally referred to by their Pali/Sanskrit terms depending on the Buddhist lineage. The first state, samatha, is a state of tranquility or calmness of mind. And the second, vipassana, is a state of awakening or clarity of mind. The first state, samatha, is typically translated as "stopping" (referring to the mind). Samatha is the process of stopping, calming, fully resting, and healing the mind. The growing popularity of mindfulness as a way to "manage" one's emotions and reduce stress comes from the samatha side of the equation.

Samatha, which moving forward I'll refer to as tranquility or calmness of mind, is the necessary basis for the second stage, vipassana, which refers to seeing deeply or with clarity. The English equivalent of vipassana is "insight", and it's the word typically associated with vipassana. Insight is *wisdom gained through direct experience*, and insight into the "true nature of reality" is what vipassana is all about (moving forward I'll refer to vipassana as insight or clarity of mind). You're likely familiar with the concept of "learning from experience". You know, the idea that, say, reading something in a book and "knowing" it is different from experiencing it yourself. You might have read ten books on true love and think you know all about it, but until you actually experience true love for yourself you don't really know true love. That's insight. In the case of spiritual practice though this direct experience is typically a direct experience of the "ultimate reality". This ultimate reality goes by many names: the ultimate or absolute dimension, the ground of being, or even God, depending on your interpretation. But we'll get more into that in the next chapter.

Likewise, the "benefits", or purpose, of mindfulness can be separated based on these two states as well. Which brings us to the topic of this chapter: the first "power" of mindfulness. The first power of mindfulness is **the ability to help one obtain a tranquil, or calm, mind (samatha).**

A tranquil mind is the very foundation of spiritual practice. Without it, we wouldn't be able to obtain awakening, the state of complete liberation and true happiness. How does mindfulness help us attain a tranquil mind? The process can be broken down into four components: stopping, calming, fully resting, and healing.

Stopping

Obtaining a tranquil mind, the practice of samatha, is ultimately about stopping. We need to learn how to stop. At first this might seem silly, "I'm sitting while I'm reading this book. I'm stopping!" But it's not so simple. By stopping I mean we need to stop both body and mind. A mind at rest is a peaceful mind. So we need to learn how to fully stop and let our minds calm. By doing so we bring us back to ourselves. This is called the practice of "going home", and it's the practice of going home to ourselves by reuniting mind and body. The practice of mindful breathing does just that- it allows us to reunite mind and body as they're truly meant to be. This is important because the way we typically live our lives, both mind and body are almost always separated.

Mindfulness is in opposition to the way we usually live our lives. That is, halfway in our heads, bouncing around in an endless stream of thoughts, and halfway in the present moment, only partially awake to what we're doing. This state of semi-consciousness, or mind dispersion, is a state where we're unable to attain complete rest and our minds are perpetually clouded.

This semi-conscious state, or mind dispersion, is what the Buddha often referred to as our "monkey mind". Our monkey mind is constantly bouncing from one thought to another. We're doing one thing (body) but thinking about another (mind). We're driving home from work while we're thinking about work, and then bills, and then dinner, and then that dinner date with your old friend coming up, and then your daughter's school project, and then whatever happened to your favorite band because they seemed to drop off the map, and then "When was that TV special again?", and then work, oh and then that sounds good for dinner, and then you look in your overhead mirror and think "I look tired today", and then a Sit-And-Sleep commercial for some reason pops into your head and so you start thinking about how you really should get a new mattress soon, and then you think about home again and how the day is passing so quickly, and then, and then, and then...it never ends. That is, unless you work to calm the mind.

Mindfulness delicately brings the mind to rest and reunites body and mind as one force. When you walk to work you're walking to work and you're enjoying the walk with all of your being. You're not thinking about what's for dinner or what you'll say to your boss about that project when you get into the office while walking. Your body is walking and your mind is walking. When you drive home you know you're driving. You're not letting yourself be distracted by the passing billboard advertisements or thinking about your overdue bills. You're truly enjoying the drive home in peace and quiet. When you're sitting down to play with your children you're fully present for them, giving them your complete and undivided attention. When you live with mindfulness you're able to truly appreciate the presence of your loved ones.

This state of mind dispersion does more than just make us stressed and take us away from our loved ones. On top of heightening stress and anxiety it decreases our productivity, restrains our creativity, disconnects us from the world around us, and overall makes us less happy. Instead of being at peace, our minds are in chaos. And as long as our attention is dispersed this monkey will rear its mischievous little head. The only way to stop our monkey mind is with mindfulness. Mindfulness gives us the ability to stop our monkey minds. Once we learn how to do this, the process of calming the mind, obtaining complete rest, and healing comes naturally. This is because, in reality, there's no separating the four components of a tranquil mind (samatha) as you'll see in the next few sections.

Calming

By living in the present moment with mindfulness we're able to bring our mind into a state of deep calm. A natural byproduct of learning how to stop the mind and body and simply be fully present, such as for the act of following one's breath, is a calm mind. Indeed, the opposite of our monkey mind is a calm mind.

Calming the mind is a process though. It doesn't happen all at once. We build up a lot of stress and tension in our everyday lives and it takes some time to fully calm the mind, especially assuming your current life doesn't just stop when you begin practicing mindfulness (which it doesn't!). You'll still have the same headaches and stressors as before and so you'll need to calm the mind despite these things constantly getting in the way. Of course, this is a two sided problem. You might need to reevaluate why you do certain things which are causing you stress. But your focus should always be on your practice of mindfulness. By making the act of stopping a priority and seeking to live your life fully in the present moment, cherishing every moment of life, you'll naturally begin to calm the mind.

Resting

Nowadays, we're so productivity focused we even map out our vacations. A checklist for a vacation? Yeah, we've lost our way. We live off checklists and to-do lists at work and at home. We think the more things we check off our list the better we'll feel. We don't even notice it but what we're chasing is peace. We're hoping for just a little slice of it here and there, even if it's temporary. But we don't have to settle for these temporary states of peace, we can have the whole pie. Indeed, if we could only learn how to truly come in touch with it we'd see that this pie is limitless.

We need to learn how to attain complete rest. By complete rest I'm referring to a fully rested mind and body. A state which most of us rarely if ever feel. And a full night's sleep doesn't provide this for us either. We're tossing, turning, and bending our bodies in uncomfortable positions which lead to aches and pains. To add to that we're dreaming constantly. And the more your mind is racing when you go to bed, the more it will be racing in your dreams when you go to sleep. Worst of all though, our sleep can be interrupted (especially if you have kids!). That really sets us off. Then there's the fact that sleep primarily rests the body and does very little for our monkey minds. The second we wake up, we're right back in the jungle.

Mindfulness, particularly sitting meditation, allows us to attain this state of complete rest. It gives our minds the rest it needs. My favorite example is the image of a pebble slowly falling to the ocean floor. Imagine your mind is the pebble. The longer you meditate, the deeper the pebble sinks. And the deeper the pebble sinks, the more calm and peaceful your mind becomes. Meditate until you feel your mind reach the ocean floor. Imagine your body slowly sinking just like the pebble. Then simply sit there for however long you'd like. Be fully present for this state of absolute calm. This is what tranquility feels like. This is true rest.

If we can learn how to rest in this way we give ourselves the ability to overcome so much. Without a doubt, one of the major reasons we experience so much stress and anxiety in modern life is because we don't know how to attain complete rest.

Healing

This last section is about learning how to utilize the body's natural healing ability. In order to attain a tranquil mind, it's not enough to stop, calm, and completely rest the body. These are key aspects of achieving a tranquil mind. But if we don't know how to heal our mind and body then we'll have no chance of attaining a calm mind.

Our mind and body comes equipped with a natural healing ability. We've all but forgotten about it, living in an age of advanced medicine, thousands of both over-the-counter and subscription medicines, and a whole roster of mental and physical professionals all ready to help us heal our mental and physical wounds. It's because of this that we now grossly underestimate our own ability to heal.

We've forgotten that the only thing necessary in order to heal is to *be with* that which needs to be healed. My favorite example of this is from Zen master Thich Nhat Hanh. He often speaks of how, when injured, an animal's natural instinct is to find somewhere safe and quiet to lie and rest. This is what it means to *be with* an illness, whether mental or physical. By stopping all activity the animal conserves every ounce of energy. This puts all of their being into the process of healing. You can do this yourself to heal both mental and physical illness.

What is a mental illness? In the case of the mind, this could be a deep-seated negative emotion or limiting belief. Maybe you hold a deep sense of resentment, and maybe even anger, towards your spouse. Years ago, when you first started dating, things were great. You were both young and you had the entire world at your fingertips. You had fun and generally lived life with wild abandon. But years later you become married, have children, and gain multiple responsibilities. Now you feel as if the entire world has closed in around you. You feel like all the opportunity and possibilities that were once at your fingertips are all but gone, never to return. Because of this, you now resent your spouse. You see them as the very source of your suffering. They didn't necessarily do anything wrong, but you created these "mental formations" of resentment and anger and labelled them the cause. This is an example of a very deep-seated emotion which needs to be overcome in order to achieve tranquility.

In order to heal this and any other form of deep-seated emotion you need to sit in meditation and simply be with the emotion. When mindful, you awaken and see through all illusions. Your limiting beliefs rise to the surface. This allows your body and mind's natural healing process to take effect. You simply need to care for the emotion. Tend to it. Accept it fully with compassion. Much of our suffering comes from our tendency to bottle up emotions and ignore them, thinking that if we do they'll go away. But this never happens. Neglect won't heal your wounds. You need to face these emotions with your mindfulness and self-compassion. Know that you're human and everyone has emotions such as these. Accept it fully with your mindfulness and it will subside. This is our natural healing ability and anyone can utilize this with practice.

As you can see, there's really no separating these four areas from each other. Stopping and calming essentially always happen simultaneously to some extent, resting involves stopping, calming, healing can really be considered a form of resting (or vice versa), and all four can be a part of one single mindfulness practice.

Finding Peace in the Age of Distraction

Distraction is a force which takes our already dispersed attention and splits it into a million different strings. It brings our monkey mind to a whole new level. This was already touched on in the section on "Stopping", but our modern world warrants extra focus on this particular point. If it wasn't enough that our minds are already naturally inclined to this semi-conscious and stress induced state, the modern era has brought us many of the worst sources for distraction all within a matter of decades.

These distractions, which are the substance of our monkey mind, are always within arm's reach in our modern world. Smartphones are in our pockets, desktops are at our place of work, and TVs are in our homes. It's so easy to distract ourselves from reality. But if we can bring our attention back to the present moment with mindfulness we have the ability to attain both a tranquil mind and clear vision.

This is the reason mindfulness is so attractive to us. Our modern world is plugged in 24/7 and it's difficult to get away from these distractions even if you make an effort. More than ever it's so easy to live in a mindless and disconnected state of being. Most of us are rarely fully present. We live in a state of perpetual distraction. We live the majority of our lives in one place while thinking of another. We're at work but we're thinking about what to make for dinner tonight at home. We're at home thinking about that project we have to finish at work. We're enjoying eating out with our family but we're really inside of our heads, stressing about the bills we have to pay next month. We all think this is normal. That it's OK. But it's not. This mind dispersion is the cause of much of our suffering and discontent.

After a tough day, one where you've been rushing around constantly and inevitably forgotten to take time for yourself, your mind will naturally be more active. If you sit down to meditate during this time you'll see that your mind is literally like a firecracker. It will be very difficult to keep the mind in one place for more than a few seconds. In this situation the mind will often be distracted over nothing special. It's still racing because it's conditioned to you racing around, not because there's anything particular going on in your consciousness. Mindfulness of these distractions won't lead to any great liberation. This is simply a sign that you need to slow things down. If your life continues as is, it will be very difficult to attain complete rest and fully quiet the mind. And if you can't calm the mind you certainly won't be able to get to the point where you can start gaining clarity of mind. Of course, that's part of the point of mindfulness. In the beginning, in order for you to practice mindfulness of anything you'll have to do it very slowly. If you're constantly rushing around, your mindfulness practice won't be authentic. You'll be telling yourself that you're practicing mindfulness but you won't actually be mindful.

Computers, smartphones, and TVs aren't the enemy. But you do need to be careful not to go overboard. By shining the light of mindfulness on your life you'll be able to see clearly the effect these things have on your mind and body and be able to make the right decision for your well-being and the well-being of your loved ones.

It's important to establish mindfulness as a way of life as opposed to simply "something you do sometimes". By making mindfulness a way of life you'll begin to notice how these things distract you and pull you away from the real beauty of life. You'll naturally begin to distance yourself from these devices a bit. A busy mind is only natural and the modern age has made our minds more chaotic than ever. But by developing the practice of mindfulness in your daily life you have the ability to stop, calm, fully rest, and heal the mind and body which will provide a re-newable source of peace and joy in your everyday life. In Part 3 I'll cover all the tips and tricks I've personally used to establish mindfulness as a way of life.

Awakening to Your True Nature

As we discussed in the last chapter, mindfulness can allow us to obtain a tranquil mind and thereby bring a wellspring of peace and joy into our lives. But mindfulness has another important role. *It's the energy which allows us to discover the truth.* Specifically, the true nature of things including ourselves. So the second power of mindfulness is **the ability to help one obtain perfect clarity and awaken to one's true nature (vipassana).** By true nature I'm referring to our true "way" or our natural existence. By seeking to live in this way we can move beyond wrong perceptions and discover our true selves.

To discover one's true self is something so many people strive for. Some strive to discover this elusive state most of their lives. But so many of us have no idea what exactly this entails. Where do we start? The very question of "who am I?" is as confusing as it is open ended. For the most part, this question is difficult to answer because there are so many hidden forces at work in our lives: the negative emotions which keep us locked in a perpetual "mental prison", the ego which strives to protect our self-worth at all costs, the ever-present pressure from society to conform to often unrealistic or misguided ideas, other false views which distort our perception, and worst of all: fear. Fear of everything. Fear of what people think of us, fear of losing those close to us, and fear of losing our position in life, among other things. These forces alter our perception of reality. We think that these things are "us", so the question of "who am I?" becomes a seemingly impossible and often painful question to answer. But these things aren't really us. By living with mindfulness we can see beyond these wrong perceptions to our true nature.

What is our true nature? It's beyond all perception, beyond all mental formations, beyond the physical body we inhabit, and beyond the sense organs we use to experience the world around us. And it's beyond consciousness. You're not your thoughts, emotions, or sensations. Sure, you are a separate body, a separate brain, and you exist in a very real way separate from those around you. But at the same time you're not a separate self, disconnected from everything and everyone around you. You're limitless. You're in the trees, the flowers, and the clouds. And these things are in you. To confine ourselves to a limited identity such as "I am this old, this nationality, this sex, good at this, bad at this, I work here, and I've accomplished this." is to confine ourselves inside of a small box. Our true nature is boundless. We're intrinsically connected to all living and nonliving things. We and everything around us is impermanent, and yet, we exist beyond life and death itself in an endless continuation of energy. Our true existence is within the very ground of being, the plane of existence beyond words in which all things exist as one.

The essence of discovering our true nature is to come in contact with the ultimate. What is that? It goes by many names- the ultimate reality, the ultimate dimension, the ground of being, Buddha mind, nirvana, and even God. The ground of being is the ultimate level of reality. It can't be completely described in words because it's beyond the concept of language. It can only be experienced. It exists in some form in just about every religion and spiritual tradition on Earth. I don't want to speak too much about it, but know that the ultimate purpose of all spiritual practice is to touch the ground of being. *By living deeply in this world, the historical reality, we can touch the ground of being or ultimate reality.* To touch the historical reality deeply is a very meaningful and fulfilling practice. You don't need anything else. In that moment, everything is perfect. And you realize what true happiness is. *To discover our true nature is in fact to discover our true selves and our true potential.*

Building a resting place

It's important to become aware of the ideas in this chapter, but if you're just starting out don't bother with awakening or any of this ultimate reality stuff. Just focus on calming the mind. Work on stopping, calming, fully resting, and healing as we spoke about in the last chapter. Develop your mindfulness practice by sitting, walking, breathing, and doing as many basic tasks throughout your day with mindfulness. Do this for at least a few months. Let your practice progress naturally.

As we spoke about in the last chapter, with time you'll develop a great feeling of calm, experience a strong sense of peace and joy in everyday life, obtain complete rest, and heal the mind. These are all very important. But it also takes time to develop mindfulness as an ability and as a habit, so don't try to rush through this part. You won't get anywhere if you rush and will just end up wasting a lot of time and effort. The practice of calming the mind never ends, it will be something you practice for the rest of your life and it's equally important to gaining clarity of mind. Don't think you can bypass this and become truly at peace without it. There's no separating the two states of samatha and vipassana, in reality *they're two sides of the same coin.*

Remember when I said that calming the mind was the foundation for obtaining a clear mind? Tranquility and clarity are natural extensions of one another. When we calm our mind, it's like we've built a nest for our mind. This nest nurtures and heals the mind naturally. This is our resting place. But this resting place is also fertile ground for receiving insight. Take the time to build this resting place and you'll have a strong foundation which will allow you to begin touching reality deeply.

There's no separating the two states of samatha and vipassana, in reality they're two sides of the same coin.

Shining the Light of Mindfulness

So how does mindfulness help us discover our true nature? Mindfulness is the very vehicle which helps us see reality in its true state. By learning to live with mindfulness we can develop great clarity in order to see the world as it is. By "as it is", I'm referring to seeing into the true nature of all things. This is reality in its true form, free from our wrong views. And the act of obtaining this great mental clarity is traditionally called "awakening" (or "enlightenment" in many English translations of ancient Buddhist text). Why is all this important? Because it's through this process of awakening that we discover our true nature and experience the ground of being. And it's only until we learn to touch the ground of being that we discover the ultimate level of inner peace.

Imagine an orange. Your whole life you've seen this orange and you think the way that you see it is the way that it is. But, as we spoke about earlier, our wrong views color the lens (our perception) with which we perceive reality through. This wrong view of reality, which can be caused by a combination of "mental formations" such as fear, anger, and ignorance among many other things, is the ultimate source of all our suffering. By suffering I'm referring to a sort of mental ill-being. Think of it as the opposite of inner peace. With mindfulness the true nature of the orange will gradually reveal itself. You'll see the orange peel back its skin and reveal something completely different from what you had perceived before. This is the process of awakening to the true nature of things.

Just as with calming the mind, gaining clarity of mind is a process. Don't expect some sudden enlightenment to happen one day while practicing mindfulness. Moments of clarity can happen. These are moments of insight. But awakening is the slow process of peeling yourself and everything else in the world back one piece at a time to unveil the truth. You've lived your whole life "collecting" these false views (remember the internal check point?). Imagine if you could wear ten pairs of sunglasses at once. Ten lenses, one in front of the other, in a row. Each of these lenses is a different color- green, pink, red, black- and each represents a wrong perception or mental formation which blocks you from experiencing reality in its true state. Your job is to remove each lens, one by one, until all ten pairs of sunglasses are gone. Each lens is blocking you from experiencing the full magnificence of the light. But with each pair of glasses you remove the more clearly you can see the light. It will take time to free yourself from all the things coloring your perception. But this is the ultimate liberation. This is true freedom. To be free from all false views, to no longer be tortured by deep-seated issues or controlled by the ego, and to realize our limitless potential. I give this example to show that clarity is a gradual process. But as you work to wipe away your false views you'll develop a great sense of peace and liberation. It doesn't just come at the end of removing the last pair of sunglasses. You experience greater peace and joy each time you remove a lens. Every moment of mindfulness is an opportunity to touch the ground of our being. This is the magic of living deeply.

To live deeply is ultimately what a spiritual practice is about. This is because to live deeply is to touch the ground of being and eventually be liberated of all afflictions. Living deeply means nothing is trivial. Every single action, no matter how minor, holds great significance. Living in such a way, you appreciate every little thing in your life. You appreciate the water you have to drink, the food on your plate, the clothes on your back, for having healthy eyes with which to see, and you appreciate the *absence* of all those things which you really rather not have. Living deeply, in a way that cultivates a deep appreciation for the world around you, is a very fulfilling practice. By letting our mindfulness guide us, that is, being fully present for every action and placing our entire being into everything we do, we can realize our true nature.

Mindfulness is itself our "true vision". Remember the field of mindfulness example I gave earlier? Mindfulness is the quiet observer of everything. It judges nothing, so it sees with absolute clarity. It sees the outside world, the mind *in mind* (observing ones thoughts), and it sees the mind *in things*, that is, our perception of the things we experience in the outside world. So mindfulness *is itself* awakening. When you're practicing mindfulness *you are awakened.* It will take time though to identify and realize your true nature. But know that there is nothing to be gained, nothing you need to accomplish. You're perfect just as you are *in this moment.* So to live deeply with mindfulness is to strive to live true to our nature and touch the seed of awakening in us.

How do we live deeply with mindfulness? This will be a natural progression of your mindfulness practice. Once you've become fully rested your mind will be able to rest *in mind.* You'll now be able to experience mindfulness of the mind *in the mind* and the mind *in things.* Previously, we discussed the fact that everything we see, everything we experience, passes through our perception before we experience it. Because of this, the mind itself is part of what we're experiencing. This is mindfulness of the mind *in the mind.* In simple terms, there's no escaping the mind because *the mind is us.* So when we observe the behavior of the mind with mindfulness that's mindfulness of the mind while in the mind. We think we're looking at a book, but in reality we're looking at *our perception* of the book. This is because, in reality, there is no separating subject and object. You can never separate mind from that which the mind is perceiving. What you think of the book- whether you like the book or not, think the cover looks funny or cool, or if the book conjures some sort of old memories good or bad- arises from the mind and becomes your perception of the book. So to be mindful of the book is also to be mindful of the mind *in the book*. Further-more, this means that what we perceive isn't necessarily the real world at all. The book that we see is first and foremost an object of our consciousness. When you and I look at the book, we see two different books. I might have a bad memory of the book which distorts my perception of it. On the other hand, you might have a *good* memory of the book with positively distorts your perception of it. Neither is correct, *they're both distorted perceptions of the book.* It's when we can see the true book that we experience our own true nature.

Mindfulness is our master tool in the study of the self. By developing the power of mindfulness to the point where we can experience the mind in mind and the mind in things we begin to see that everything is mind. If the book we see (not the real book) is really an object of our consciousness, and the process of gain-ing clarity of mind is really about extinguishing all false views such as these, then mindfulness' role is the tool which allows us to see deeply into ourselves and identify these false views. The light of mindfulness, the great observer, is also a great healer. Remember the animal that simply sits and rests in peace and quiet in order to heal its wounds? Mindfulness is the healing energy which allows us to gradually erode all false views and concepts in order to touch the ground of our being. To realize our true nature is the only way to experience true inner peace. It will be difficult at first, but if you let mindfulness be your guide it will lead you to an existence filled with peace and joy.

Part 2
Practicing Mindfulness

Mindful Sitting

In Zen, the practice of sitting meditation is called "zazen", which literally means sitting or seated meditation in Japanese. Zen monks practice zazen for long hours each day, even occasionally having meditation marathons where practitioners meditate for two-thirds to half of an entire day for multiple days straight. Why do Zen Buddhists put so much of their focus on sitting meditation? Because sitting meditation is the very foundation of meditative practice.

Think of a professional athlete. Despite being the best in the world at what they do, nearly every single day they practice the most fundamental aspects of their practice. Not only that, they do it for long hours. A professional and even championship winning NBA basketball player will continue to practice lay ups, jump shots, running up and down the court, passing the ball, running basic plays, as well as free throws constantly. This is the very essence of someone who has committed themselves to being the best at what they do. The essence of the greatest performers in the world in all callings. It's the very drilling of these fundamental principles that is what makes them so great. To lose sight of the core or fundamental practices which constitute your endeavor is to lose sight of your practice. Likewise, by practicing mindful sitting every day you make it easier to call upon your mindfulness during the rest of your day. If you'd like to establish a solid foundation in your mindfulness practice then setting up a daily practice of sitting meditation, either in the morning, night, or both, is very important. Mindful sitting is the foundation of the rest of your mindfulness practice. You don't have to meditate for long hours though. You can start off by meditating for as little as 5 minutes a day and work your way up.

Zazen, or sitting meditation, is where I first started my own mindfulness practice. At first, without anyone there to coach or teach me, I thought the amount of activity in my head while meditating was abnormal. I was surprised with how chaotic my mind was and couldn't believe that I had been living like that, without ever giving my mind a rest. Little did I know at the time that what was going on in my head was perfectly normal. I was merely experiencing the typical monkey mind, which everyone experiences. But it didn't take long to get my mind to a relatively calm state. And as this happened, something began to develop inside of me. I'd feel it strongest during and right after my meditation session, but it started extending throughout the rest of my day gradually. It's one of the greatest feelings I've ever experienced in my life, but it's hard to explain. Simply "peaceful" is probably the best word to use. You need nothing during those moments of meditation. Everything is perfectly peaceful and you feel as if you could sit forever. Not every meditation session will be like this. Even after working to calm the mind for some time you'll occasionally experience a tough day or a tough week and struggle during meditation. If this happens you just need to stick with it. Turn up the volume on your practice even, meditate for longer or do an extra session on that day or during that tough week in order to handle the pressure. If you persist, you'll overcome it and arrive at a point where you can keep your mind in a calm state even despite tough times. Establish a strong foundation of mindful sitting in your mindfulness practice and you'll be rewarded with a stability that nothing can shake. Like a tree that stands tall in a strong wind, nothing will be able to knock you down.

How to practice mindful sitting

The below instructions are separated into three sections: sitting, breathing, and finally meditating. The first section "Sit" goes over adopting the optimal posture and positioning. The second section "Breathe" covers how to properly follow and count your breath during meditation. Lastly, the third section "Be Mindful" goes over how to use your mindfulness while sitting. Keep in mind that while there may be ten (simple) steps, ultimately the practice of mindful sitting is as simple as one, two, and three: 1) sit down, 2) follow your breath, and 3) acknowledge anything and everything that steps into your field of mindfulness (or in other words, anything that diverts your concentration).

Sit

1. **Find a quiet place:** First, find a quiet place where you won't be interrupted.

2. **Find the optimal sitting position:** Find the sitting position that's most comfortable for you. Here are the most common:

2a. **Full lotus:** If possible, sit on the floor in the full or half lotus position. The full lotus position makes your body into a tripod, making it by far the most stable or sitting positions. To sit in the full lotus position, sit down in a typical cross-legged position. Now, take your left leg and place it on top of your right thigh (closer to your waist than your knee). Next, take your right leg and place it on top of you left thigh. This second leg will be much more difficult than the first. While moving the left leg make sure that the right leg does not slip from its position. While keeping your body in place, slide your bottom back a little to straighten your back.

2b. Half-lotus: The full lotus can be a difficult position to sit in, especially at first. In that case, you might feel more comfortable starting with the half lotus. In order to sit in the half lotus position, just place your left leg over your right thigh (or right leg over your left thigh). You should alternate regularly with the right leg on the left thigh as well. Eventually, with practice, it will become comfortable.

2c. Sit in a chair: If neither of these is possible you can also sit in a chair. Make sure to plant your feet on the ground and sit with your back straight. You can place a pillow or a zafu between your lower back and and the back of the chair to keep your back straight.

2d. Use a cushion (if possible): Whether you sit in the full lotus, half, lotus, a simple cross-legged position, or choose to use a chair I'd suggest using a firm pillow or a zafu (a Zen meditation pillow). A zafu pillow really improves stability, posture, and overall comfort during sitting meditation. Just sit on the last third or so of the zafu or firm pillow in order to help straighten your back (you can fold a typical bed pillow in half and sit on that if you don't have either). If you're sitting in the full or half lotus this will also help bring both knees to the floor, creating the tripod I spoke about in the full lotus section. Unless you do this one knee will stick up slightly while you're in the full or half lotus position, sacrificing some stability and comfort. A cushion isn't necessary, it just makes meditation more comfortable and therefore allows you to focus more on what's important: your meditation.

3. Loosen up: Now that you're in your optimal seated position, relax and take a few deep breaths. Stretch your back, neck, shoulders, and arms a bit. Loosen the muscles in your face by forming a half-smile. Feel all of the tension roll off your body.

Relaxing your body will make it easier to focus during your meditation.

4. Form the proper posture: This is very important in meditation (actually it's always important). Improper posture can cause you back pain, obstruct your breathing and even affect your concentration, so make sure to take the time to perfect the proper sitting meditation posture. Your back and neck should be straight with the top of your head pointed towards the sky. Let your stomach relax. If you tilt your chin just slightly you will gain greater stability as well. Also, if you're on a zafu or firm pillow you can rock back and forth as well as left and right in order to find the most stable position for your body. If your posture is solid but you're leaning a bit on your pillow your muscles will stay tensed trying to balance you on the pillow. By rocking you can find the most stable position and remove that potential distraction during meditation.

5. Form the cosmic mudrā: Mudrā is a Sanskrit word meaning "seal", "mark", or "gesture". A mudrā is essentially a placement of the body which is supposed to symbolize some greater principle and remind the practitioner of that principle, although I believe the original purpose of mudras was also to improve the flow of oxygen to the body by adopting optimal positioning of the hands and arms. Because my background is in Zen Buddhist meditation, I form the "cosmic" mudrā while meditating. In order to form the cosmic mudrā, place your hands in your lap with palms facing up. Place one hand on top of the other, the dominant hand's finger joints on top of the other hand's finger joints so that your dominant hand's fingers overlap the other hands. Thumbs touching at the tips creating an oval shape inside of your hands. The purpose of the cosmic mudrā is to place your focus on the "hara", or spiritual center of the body, which is located about 2 inches below your naval. Placing the hara as your point of attention brings mind, body and breath together as one and assists you in following your breath.

6. **Eyes half-closed:** Look down a couple of feet in front of you and then let your eyelids drop naturally. They should end up about halfway shut. The reason you keep your eyes partially open is so as to not invite lethargy and doze off. You look down because it helps your eyelids lower naturally which also keeps you from blinking as often.

Breathe

7. **Be mindful of your in breath and out breath:** Close your mouth and breathe in and out through your nose. If a cold or some other condition makes this uncomfortable then it's OK to breathe through your mouth, although deeper and more effortless breathing can be done through the nostrils. Breathe in, breathe out. Put complete focus on your breath. Your breath is your singular focus during this meditation. Don't attempt to control your breath, simply observe it silently. Your silent observation will slowly begin to calm your breathing naturally. Feel your breath gradually go in and out. In order to keep your concentration on your breath you'll need to follow each complete in breath and out breath from start to finish. This will also make it easier to notice when you've lost your concentration and give you a clear path to regain it. You should be attempting to be mindful of your breath 100% of the time you're sitting.

8. **Count each inhalation and exhalation:** Inhale...one. Exhale....two. Count the number at the end each inhale and exhale. Count to 10 like this. If a thought distracts you, start the 10 count over from 1. When you get to 10, start over and attempt to count to 10 again. Do this for as many weeks or months as it

54

takes *until you can count to 10 repeatedly with little effort.* Then count each inhale + exhale as one. Then, when that becomes easy, stop counting and simply follow your breath. *Don't rush this step, progress naturally.* This step is incredibly important in the beginning stages because this is how you'll develop your power of concentration.

Be Mindful

9. **Gently acknowledge any thoughts and feelings:** Thoughts will come, don't push them away. Noticing this is a good thing, it means your mindfulness is developing. Remember that these thoughts, feelings, and sensations are natural. Meditation is acceptance, not avoidance. You want those things to rise to the surface during meditation because that is when the real healing will begin. Fear, anger, stress, and so many other things can and will rise to the surface so that you can let them run their course and dissipate. Each one of these afflictions you heal will bring you greater peace and happiness.

10. **Immediately recapture focus on your breath:** Let go of the thought and return to your breath. This will be difficult at first, you'll lose focus constantly. Don't become frustrated when your mind drifts, know that it's a normal part of the process. Stay focused, after a while your mind will begin to grow quieter and you'll start gaining better control over your mind. This may take a few weeks or even months.

Once you're done meditating, don't rush off. Sit for another few seconds or so and slowly release your legs so that they can stretch if you were sitting in one of the lotus positions. At first the full lotus might make one of your legs fall asleep. You'll just have to get used to this sitting position. The nice thing is, you won't feel it until you undo your legs at the end of your session. But it's a wonderful feeling (joke)! And lastly, take a few seconds to relish this moment of peace and feel the difference in your mind and body before getting up and continuing on with your day.

In the beginning, you'll want to meditate for 5-10 minutes at a time once or twice a day. Increase your sessions by about 5 minutes at a time whenever you feel comfortable. You should feel gradually able to sit down for longer and longer periods. Work your way up to whatever timetable is best for you, but if you'd like a recommendation I'd say somewhere around two 30-45 minute sessions per day. Remember though, that it's up to you. Meditate for however long you want, just remember that the longer you meditate the more beneficial it will be.

Mindful Walking

We walk to our cars, to work, to home, stores, and sometimes just for fun. Wherever you are and whenever you walk you almost always have the opportunity to make it a mindful walk. There's so many great opportunities to practice mindful walking in the average person's day that it can be adopted by anyone with little effort and create a major impact on one's sense of inner peace.

Mindful walking is generally considered one of the core meditative practices. But traditionally, mindful walking is called walking meditation. Don't get confused though, when I say walking meditation I'm simply talking about mindful walking. Walking meditation has been practiced by people of various spiritual traditions for possibly as long as sitting meditation. This is probably because of how natural, simple, and nourishing the practice of walking meditation is. While practicing walking meditation your object of concentration is your steps. First, concentrate on the foot rising and being placed down onto the ground. Once the foot has been placed down you shift your concentration to the second foot doing the same motion. At first, you'll have to practice walking meditation very slowly to get the hang of it. But after a while, as with anything else in mindfulness, you'll be able to walk mindfully at a normal speed while staying mindful. The act of placing your foot down on the ground can be done in a very deep way. By acknowledging the earth's presence below your foot each time you place your foot down you can experience a deep sense of peace and joy in the simple act of walking.

How to Practice Mindful Walking

Decide

1. **Decide where you're walking to:** Fix your sights on a location in front of you such as your car, your house, a building, the end of a room, a street, or a tree. Wherever it is, decide consciously that this is where you're walking to before you begin walking mindfully.

Walk

2. **Match your steps with your breath:** Breathe naturally, see how many slow steps you take for each natural inhale and exhale. This step can be difficult at first because you'll want to control your breathing or your steps. Don't attempt to control either. Resist trying to control both your breathing and your steps and let them flow naturally.

3. **Be mindful of your steps:** As I mentioned earlier, the object of your concentration in this meditation will be your steps. Put 100% of your concentration into your steps. You'll want to put great care into each step you take, so walk slowly. Feel one foot rise and then come down. As soon as that foot is placed down be mindful of your other foot rising up and then coming down as well. Then back to the first foot, and the next, and the next. Move slowly and shift your concentration back and forth from one foot to the other. In order to keep your concentration on your steps you'll need to follow each complete step from start to finish. This will also make it easier to notice when you've lost your concentration and give you a clear path to regain it.

4. Count each step: Just as you count your breaths in sitting meditation, you can say "in" for each step on inhale and "out" for each step on exhale. So "in, in, in" on each inhale if you take 3 steps and "out, out, out" on each exhale for 3 more in order to improve your ability to notice when you lose your concentration. You can also say a phrase that calms you if you prefer. In that case, just match the number of steps you're taking with syllables. So 3 steps per inhale/exhale could be "be-at-peace".

Be Mindful

5. Gently acknowledge any thoughts and feelings: Thoughts will come, don't push them away. Noticing this is a good thing, it means your mindfulness is developing. Remember that these thoughts, feelings, and sensations are natural. Meditation is acceptance, not avoidance. You want those things to rise to the surface during meditation because that is when the real healing will begin. Fear, anger, stress, and so many other things can and will rise to the surface so that you can let them run their course and dissipate. Each one of these afflictions you heal will bring you greater peace and happiness.

6. Immediately recapture focus on your breath: Let go of the thought and return to your breath. This will be difficult at first, you'll lose focus constantly. Don't become frustrated when your mind drifts, know that it's a normal part of the process. Stay focused, after a while your mind will begin to grow quieter and you'll start gaining better control over your mind. This may take a few weeks or even months.

Take this moment in for everything that it is. There is no past and no future. Know that peace exists in this moment as you walk across the earth in mindfulness. Feel the earth beneath your feet. Whether you're walking on grass, sand, pavement, or dirt, know that you're touching mother earth deeply with each step. The same mother earth that every one of your ancestors walked on before you. Walking meditation is a special practice which should be treated with great care. As little as 15 minutes of mindful walking can completely transform the stress of your day into pure peace.

Walk mindfully everywhere you go. Anytime you can, take a second to walk in mindfulness. Take a second to look around and appreciate your surroundings. Take a mindful breath of fresh air. Then go back to your steps. In this moment, you're truly awake and touching the depths of your being.

Mindful Breathing

Mindful sitting is essentially mindful breathing, but there's a distinct difference between sitting in a quiet room and pooling all of your concentration towards meditation vs. stopping at various points in your busy day to come back to yourself through mindful breathing. Both are mindful breathing, but this chapter will show you how to explore the latter. Mindful breathing is the practice of "going home". By going home I mean coming back to yourself and uniting body and mind. This is a very important practice. Many people today are rushing around so much that they don't stop all day to rest until it's time for bed. I know the feeling. You want to be as productive as possible, and you convince yourself that you'll be fine no matter how hard you push yourself. But you aren't, and you won't be. You're making yourself stressed, anxious, unhappy, easy to anger, easy to distract, less effective, less productive, and muffling your creativity by pushing yourself so hard. And it will only get worse. *You need to learn the art of stopping and breathing.* This is the practice of mindful breathing. Mindful breathing can be a very nourishing practice if you work on developing it. It can work like an anchor in your life, keeping you grounded no matter what is going on around you. It can also work as an "emergency button" of sorts for when you encounter high stress situations.

Daily Breathing

The first way mindful breathing can be useful is as a constant companion during your daily life. We're often moving so quickly that we stop noticing what's going on around and inside

of us. In a way, we're muffling our entire lives. This is danger-
ous, because something can be happening right under our noses
and we'd never notice it. For instance, we could be developing
a deep anger towards someone over something that happened
recently and, because we're moving constantly throughout our
day without mindfulness, we never notice it until it's a real
problem. This can be very damaging to our well-being. By stopping regularly to practice mindful breathing we shine a sort of
spotlight on our lives and give ourselves the ability to not only
detect these wounds but also give ourselves a way to heal them.

I practice mindful breathing nearly every hour of every day
for 1-2 minutes. I've found this to be my most comfortable routine. No matter what I'm doing, I stop everything to practice
my mindful breathing. The first couple of days will be easy, but
after a while you'll likely find yourself ignoring your reminder
to practice or trying to give yourself the excuse that what you're
doing right now is too important and that you'll practice as soon
as you're done. Don't listen to these voices. Trust me, if you start
listening to them your practice will suffer and you'll notice it. I'd
say it's actually healthy for this to happen a few times at first. It
will lead you to a greater appreciation of your practice because
you'll see the difference in how you feel. But make sure to get
right back on course and use the learning experience as an opportunity to strengthen your practice.

To practice mindful breathing, you'll do essentially the same
as in the mindful sitting chapter, with just a few changes:

Stop

1. **Stop:** Stop everything. If you're at work you might prefer to find a more private place. In my experience though if you
just stop and breathe where you're at it will just look like you're
standing or sitting in your normal way. No one will notice. You

can stare at your computer screen or desk if you're sitting for instance. You'll typically only stop to breathe for a minute or so anyway so it will be pretty quick.

Breathe

2. **Be mindful of your in breath and out breath:** Close your mouth and breathe in and out through your nose. If a cold or some other condition makes this uncomfortable then it's OK to breathe through your mouth, although deeper and more effortless breathing can be done through the nostrils. Breathe in, breathe out. Put complete focus on your breath. Your breath is your singular focus during this meditation. Don't attempt to control your breath, simply observe it silently. Your silent observation will slowly begin to calm your breathing naturally. Feel your breath gradually go in and out. In order to keep your concentration on your breath you'll need to follow each complete in breath and out breath from start to finish. This will also make it easier to notice when you've lost your concentration and give you a clear path to regain it. You should be attempting to be mindful of your breath 100% of the time you're sitting.

3. **Count each inhalation and exhalation:** Inhale…one. Exhale….two. Count the number at the end of each inhale and exhale. Count to 10 like this. If a thought distracts you, start the 10 count over from 1. When you get to 10, start over and attempt to count to 10 again. Do this for as many weeks or months as it takes *until you can count to 10 repeatedly with little effort.* Then count each inhale + exhale as one. Then, when that becomes easy, stop counting and simply follow your breath. *Don't rush this step, progress naturally.* This step is incredibly important in the beginning stages because this is how you'll develop your power of concentration.

Be Mindful

4. **Gently acknowledge any thoughts and feelings:** Thoughts will come, don't push them away. Noticing this is a good thing, it means your mindfulness is developing. Remember that these thoughts, feelings, and sensations are natural. Meditation is acceptance, not avoidance. You want those things to rise to the surface during meditation because that is when the real healing will begin. Fear, anger, stress, and so many other things can and will rise to the surface so that you can let them run their course and dissipate. Each one of these afflictions you heal will bring you greater peace and happiness.

5. **Immediately recapture focus on your breath:** Let go of the thought and return to your breath. This will be difficult at first, you'll lose focus constantly. Don't become frustrated when your mind drifts, know that it's a normal part of the process. Stay focused, after a while your mind will begin to grow quieter and you'll start gaining better control over your mind. This may take a few weeks or even months.

Do this for about sixty seconds. You don't have to time yourself though unless you prefer to. Just breathe mindfully for what feels like about a minute. It's easy to set a quick timer with your phone though if you'd rather be exact. I'd test both out and see what works better. The main reason you might end up preferring to not set a timer is because it's generally best to practice your short mindful breathing session for as long as it takes you to get to a semi-deep state of meditation. This could take thirty seconds, one minute, sometimes two. Personally, I go without a timer. If it takes me two minutes to bring relative calm to myself it usually means I'm a little busier than normal. In which case, I'd prefer to breathe a little bit longer.

Emergency Button

Another way to use mindful breathing is as a sort of "emergency button". What I mean by that is if you encounter a high stress situation, such as when receiving some bad news, you can use mindful breathing to stop and calm your mind in order to take hold of yourself during this difficult situation. Our breath is a powerful force. It can be used to control our very emotions. When you're feeling an intense anxiety, fear, anger, or sadness you can use mindful breathing to calm the feeling and literally take back control of the situation. Don't underestimate the power of your breathing. Your breath is one of your greatest tools in controlling your mood, use it often and wisely.

Remember when I mentioned the importance of breathing mindfully until you feel a relative calm come over you as opposed to sticking to a set timer? The only difference between practicing mindful breathing throughout your day and mindful breathing in "emergency" situations is that you'll always want to breathe until the point in which you feel the emotion start to subside. It doesn't have to go away completely, just enough to where you can take back control of your mind (although honestly, if you have time to go sit down and breathe mindfully it will help the situation even more). However long that takes, just keep breathing. Our breath is the pathway that reunites body and mind and brings harmony to the whole. Use this amazing tool whenever you need it. The great thing is, it's always available to you. No matter where you are, no matter what you're doing, and no matter what's going on, your breath is always there to help.

Mindful Living

Mindful sitting, mindful walking, and mindful breathing are the most basic meditative practices. Going back to the example of the professional athlete, these are your fundamentals. But in order to develop a healthy practice which leads to true peace and happiness one should strive to live each waking moment in mindfulness. This will be difficult, but no matter what stage you're at the more you work at it the more rewarding your practice will be.

So, where do you start? You've got your regular morning and/or evening practice of mindful sitting, you practice your breathing every hour and you use it when you're faced with any difficult situation, and you practice mindful walking whenever possible. But when you work, sit down to eat, go out to have fun with friends or family, clean the house, or do anything else you can and should also be mindful. Every moment of every day is an opportunity to shine the healing light of mindfulness as well as to feel the peace and joy of living fully in the present moment.

Mindful eating

With multiple opportunities to practice mindful eating each day, learning to eat with mindfulness can become a very nourishing practice. Eating is already typically enjoyable, but eating with mindfulness can turn breakfast, lunch, or dinner into a deeply spiritual and joy filled experience. And anything which is naturally enjoyable can easily be done with mindfulness. This is because joy and excitement naturally pull our attention to the thing we're enjoying or are excited about and away from any potential distractions.

To practice mindful eating you simply need to direct your mindfulness to the act of chewing your food. The anchor point of mindfulness (what your concentration latches onto) is always an action executed by you. This could be breathing, walking, chewing, or a million other actions. Whatever it is, in order to be mindful you need only drop your anchor onto whatever you're doing in the present moment in order to be mindful of the entire moment. You're being mindful of both the act of placing the food into your mouth, and when it hits your mouth, the act of chewing the food itself. That's where your concentration should rest. Be fully present for the act of consuming your meal with mindfulness and everything that arises from that including the sensations of eating the food itself.

Take your time with each bite. Don't eat another bite until you're done with the bite in your mouth. If you go to take or prepare another bite before finishing the bite in your mouth then you're not eating with mindfulness. When you practice mindful eating you're being fully present for the food that's in front of you, don't try to rush through the meal in order to get to something else. This is just your conditioned mind trying to move you in the direction of your old habit energies. While you're eating with mindfulness there is nothing else. There is only the meal in front of you. To deepen your practice, take a moment to see the food in its true state. If you're eating a salad, see the lettuce leaf as the true lettuce leaf. See the water in the lettuce, the sunlight which helped the lettuce grow, the soil which provided nutrients, and the farmer who farmed the lettuce. If you took even one of these elements away the lettuce would not exist. By looking deeply into the lettuce and touching its true nature, feelings of gratitude and appreciation will naturally arise in you. This is using your mindfulness to look deeply into your meal. By eating in this way you can further deepen the practice of mindful eating and make it a very spiritually nourishing practice.

Mindful working

Many people around the world spend a third or more of their lives at work. This is an enormous amount of time. By practicing mindfulness at work you can find a lot joy in what you do, even in the simplest of tasks.

To practice mindful working you simply need to be fully present for the work at hand. Whether you're walking from one location to another, eating lunch, typing an email on your computer, or having a conversation with someone, do so with mindfulness. The next time you step into the office, don't worry about actually being mindful, simply take the day to notice opportunities to practice mindfulness. Remember every moment is an opportunity to practice mindfulness, but what you're doing here is looking for clear and easy opportunities to practice. You might work at an office, on a construction site, in a factory, or at home taking care of your children. You'll need to examine your own days to find the best times to begin introducing the practice of mindfulness into your work day and the rest of your daily life.

Most workplaces have a tendency to be busy and filled with constant distractions. So to practice mindfulness at work can also mean you need to be mindful of any unexpected occurrences that arise. Surprises are commonplace in many workplaces, so you need to know how to respond to these surprises with mindfulness. Imagine these surprises as thoughts arising while sitting in meditation. You don't push these thoughts away, you acknowledge them with your mindfulness just as you acknowledge your breath. Take care of the interruption, but always bring your focus back to the main task at hand just as when bringing your focus back to your breath. Don't let yourself be led away by distractions. This can help make you more productive as well as lend to your mindfulness practice.

Mindful experiencing

The very essence of mindfulness is to fully experience what's occurring in the present moment. When you go out with friends or spend a day with family you can practice mindful experiencing and not only continue your mindfulness practice but really take the most from the experience. Mindful experiencing is really just practicing mindfulness in general, but it's with the greater goal of making the most of time with friends and family.

During a mindful experience you could be mindful of the feeling of the breeze on your face and in your hair when driving to your destination, of how your child's smile makes you feel when doing something they enjoy, you could practice deep listening and loving speech (mindfulness of speaking and listening in conversation) while conversing with friends and family on the outing, or select a specific sense organ, such as your ears at one point and eyes on another, and simply focus on everything coming into that sense organ during those moments. If you're practicing mindfulness of hearing while taking a tram ride you can block everything out and just be mindful of every sound that enters your ears. Be fully present for every sound. If you're on a roller coaster or some amusement park ride you can practice mindfulness of body and fully take in all the twists, turns, and drops. And you don't have to do something fast paced, you could simply walk through a park with a loved one or draw with your child in mindfulness. There's a limitless number of ways you can practice mindfulness when enjoying time with friends and family. The point is that you're fully awake to whatever is happening in the present moment.

I visited Disneyland recently. I grew up near this particular Disneyland so I've been to it on a number of occasions growing up. I'm always interested to see the way people act when going out to have fun at places like amusement parks. Especially families going as a group, but not excluding anyone else. I was in line at what I believe was the Star Wars ride when my awareness was piqued by a conversation that a mother was having with her two children in front of us in line. It went something like this:

Child: "I want to go on the X ride!"
Mother: "Alright. Your brother likes this ride so we're going to get this over with and then we'll run over to X and get that over with so we have them out of the way. That way, we don't have to deal with them for the rest of the day."

It might have seemed to some like the mother was physically at Disneyland, but in reality she was still working. Ready to tackle her to-do list for the day, maximize her productivity, and keep her house or office in order. There's nothing inherently wrong with a to-do list. But so many of us get into the trap of letting a productivity mindset control our lives. We're so used to rushing around all the time thinking that if we get more done we'll be happier. But it doesn't work that way. Take your time, don't rush through these experiences just to try and get the most things done in a day. You'll only end up dead tired by the end of it and feeling like you just worked an overtime shift at work. This isn't relaxation at all. Don't forget why you go out to do things with family and friends- to enjoy yourself and each other's company. Let your mindfulness guide you towards a more enjoyable experience. It doesn't matter if you went on two rides all day, or if all you did was sit down to draw with your daughter at home. If you did it with mindfulness then it was worth more than an entire day at Disneyland.

Mindful cleaning

One of the beautiful things about mindfulness is that it can take typically boring and mundane activities and make them meaningful and deeply enjoyable. This is probably best exemplified with cleaning in mindfulness. Cleaning with mindfulness can be a very deep practice. Indeed, practices which you wouldn't typically consider deep or meaningful at all can be some of the deepest and most meaningful because of their simple nature.

What does mindful cleaning look like? It could be sweeping in mindfulness. Focusing on your body creating each stroke of the broom's brush, handling the broom and the task of sweeping with great care and reverence as if sweeping this floor was the most important thing in the universe. It could be washing dishes in mindfulness. Take the time to wash each dish with all of your being, concentrating on the act of washing the dish with your hands. If could also be mindfulness of watering the garden, cleaning the windows or tabletops, or mopping the floor. Whatever it is, while cleaning treat that particular task as the most important thing in the world at that very moment. And as usual, if you become distracted, simply acknowledge the distraction with your mindfulness and bring your concentration back to the task at hand.

Mindful living

In this chapter we've looked at mindful eating, mindful working, mindful experiencing, and mindful cleaning. Combined with mindful sitting, mindful walking, and mindful breathing we've covered huge ground. But it doesn't stop there. As I mentioned before, you can practice mindfulness of anything and everything. You should strive to be mindful 24/7. All day, every day.

The instructions we covered throughout this section can be applied towards anything. Pick your object of mindfulness, preferably some part of you *in action* because to concentrate on something stationary is much more difficult than something which is constantly changing or moving in some fashion (think in/out breath, steps, sensations, chewing and tasting, sweeping, etc.), and then simply be mindful. It might take a while to bring mindfulness into your entire life, but if you practice the fundamentals daily, keep learning, and let the light of mindfulness spread into the other areas of your life then you'll develop a practice which nurtures a deep sense of peace and happiness within you.

Part 3
Developing Mindfulness

Overcoming Old Habits

Mindfulness is like anything else, it takes work to develop it into a daily practice. You'll work and work to establish a daily practice and things will just keep getting in the way. You'll make strides but you'll also falter at times. But it will all be worth it. And with mindfulness there's no waiting for your reward, every moment in mindfulness is healing and revitalizing. In Part 3 we'll discuss the most important components to developing mindfulness as a way of life. Keep in mind that the set of tools I'll cover in this section isn't exhaustive. It's simply everything that I myself have used to develop mindfulness into a daily practice. Everyone's situation is different. You might be able to think of your own tools which will help you develop mindfulness.

What would it be like to be mindful from the time you wake up until the time you lay your head down to rest? With a daily practice of mindful sitting, mindful breathing, mindful walking, and a daily practice of showing reverence for every little moment in your daily life you'd live constantly aware of the precious nature of each moment of life, appreciative of everything you have (and don't have), calm as a gentle stream of water, with a clear vision to witness your mind unfold to the true nature of yourself and the world around you. This is the ultimate goal of all spiritual practice and ultimately what we all want. To be truly happy and at peace. That's the point.

So then what keeps us from accomplishing this? Even if you're just starting out and simply striving to meditate for 20 minutes a day, to make mindfulness a daily practice takes work. Whether your daily practice is all day, every chance you get, just sometimes, or for simply 5 minutes every day, you'll need some tools to help you develop it into a daily habit or practice. When it comes to developing mindfulness, or anything else for that matter, as a daily practice, our habit energy is the major force standing in our way. Sure, outside circumstances affect us, but without our old habit energy in the way nothing significant would hold us back from changing nearly every part of our life in an instant.

Fortunately for us, the very thing we're attempting to make a daily practice can be the most powerful force in helping us overcome old habit energies. In working to develop mindfulness as a daily practice it's important to be mindful of when your old habit energies are trying to pull you away. Simply by observing your old habit energy with mindfulness you reduce the pull it has on you. And the more you observe it the weaker it gets. Observe the old habit energy long enough without giving in and you'll transform it into something positive. When we don't *fully* know or fully realize what we're doing is bad for us then we keep doing it. This is the position so many people are in. But when we fully realize what we're doing and why it's bad for us then we stop doing that thing and almost always replace it with something positive. Mindfulness will help you delve deeply into your old habit energies and find out why you're being pulled in their direction. "I'm tired", "I don't have the energy to do that", and "I'll do it later". These are things we tell ourselves constantly in our subconscious mind without ever noticing. The longer and more often we're mindful the more we'll begin to actually witness us making these comments to ourselves. Then we'll put the power back into our own hands and be able say "no" to these many excuses. That's one of the great things about mindfulness. A lot of times all that's needed is to notice what we're really doing because we never fully see ourselves as we go about our daily lives. By seeing ourselves clearly, even without taking any particular action other than being mindful, we can rewrite these old habit energies.

But that doesn't mean that everything will be smooth sailing. No matter what you do you'll still have a lot of tough days.

Sometimes tough weeks. You'll try to practice and something will get in the way, you'll listen to your own excuses and fall off for a moment, or a number of other things that can happen will happen. No matter what you do you'll encounter adversity. So in the next two chapters of Part 3 I'll cover all of my best tips and tricks for beginning with mindfulness and establishing it as a daily practice. These are the various tools I've used to overcome my own old habit energies as well as the pull of outside circumstance to establish mindfulness as a daily practice. Each of these various tools works towards the same purpose: overcoming old habit energy and outside circumstances in order to develop mindfulness as a daily practice which nourishes your mind and body and helps you realize true peace and happiness.

Tips and Tricks for Beginning with Mindfulness

When I first started practicing mindfulness I had a lot of tough days. Sometimes a tough string of days. I'd often go the entire day and forget to practice mindfulness altogether. I knew how important it was to me and yet I'd find myself completely forgetting to be mindful all day long. It was frustrating to say the least.

By now you know why mindfulness is important, what it can do, and how to practice it. But when you actually take this information and attempt to apply it in real life you're going to see that it won't be all rainbows and cupcakes (if that's even a good thing). As with a lot of things, developing mindfulness into a regular part of your life can be difficult. Likelihood is you've already started dabbling in the techniques I spoke about in the last chapter. But in order to really develop mindfulness as a daily practice and to make it a consistent part of your life so that you reap the full benefits you need to do more than just read this book and occasionally be mindful when you remember to do so.

As we talked about earlier, modern life is filled with distractions. Not only that, we're taught to move fast, get things done quickly, and multitask whenever possible. But not only are none of these things necessarily more productive, which is the entire point, they're not generally good for our well-being and a bad environment to begin developing mindfulness in. So you're going to need some tools. At least at first, before the habit is developed. In this chapter I'm going to cover the various tools I myself used in order to develop mindfulness as a daily practice.

So, where do you start? It can be difficult to know where to begin one's practice of mindfulness. Many resources discuss mindfulness only as a form of sitting meditation. This greatly limits your practice. In order to obtain a clear mind you can't just practice mindfulness during sitting meditation. You also need to be mindful while going about your everyday life. After all, what good is anything which isn't actually useful to you in your everyday life?

One of the great things about mindfulness is that it's available to you in every moment. You can practice mindfulness right now this very second and touch seeds of peace and joy within yourself. You can directly and immediately create a positive effect in your daily life and in a number of ways. This has to be taken advantage of in order to gain the full benefit from practicing mindfulness. Sitting meditation is powerful, and in fact it's the cornerstone of meditative practice of any kind. But in order to both calm the mind and see with clarity, the two major goals of all meditation and spiritual practice, you need to also seek to be mindful during your daily routine. Not just in the morning or at night when you sit down to meditate. If you miss this you could end up with a rather unsuccessful practice and wonder what you're doing wrong.

And still others explain mindfulness in confusing jargon that only certain spiritual or religious groups can understand. Using these words can be OK. But if the author doesn't explain the meaning of the words and the purpose of mentioning them then it won't help you as the reader to understand mindfulness. It will only hurt you and turn you off to the subject. They might mean well, and the information might truly be life-changing, but if the language isn't simple and straightforward then you're just not going to bother.

But worst of all, with mindfulness' rise in popularity in the West it's easy to stumble across an incorrect explanation of how to practice mindfulness and just end up confused and unmotivated. This is the result of the age of the internet. It doesn't take an "expert" (whatever that is) to talk about mindfulness. But one thing is for certain- you shouldn't listen to anyone talk about mindfulness who hasn't made the practice of mindfulness a way of life for themselves. Unfortunately, there are a lot of people out there who seek to comment on mindfulness and profit from it due to its rise in popularity. So as you move forward be careful, and whenever possible use this book, when deciding who to listen to for advice on improving your mindfulness practice.

In order to start you off on the right foot I've organized a list of my best tips and tricks for beginning with mindfulness. These are all the things that I myself have found to be important, or made the mistake of not doing (or both), at the beginning of my own practice. Some of these have to do with adopting a particular mindset, some have to do with the way you actually practice mindfulness, and some have to do with various techniques in themselves. Following even one of these points can greatly improve your practice if you're just starting out. I'd suggest following each point closely.

Tips and tricks for beginning with mindfulness:

1. Focus on developing concentration

We've spoken about the relationship between mindfulness and concentration already, but a very important point to keep in mind is that at the beginning your mind will literally be all over the place. You'll seem to have a new thought or some other distraction every few seconds. This is perfectly normal. I went through the same thing at first. It took time to quiet my own mind, but it was well worth it. Simply quieting the mind can bring you a great sense of peace and happiness. And without calming the mind you won't be able to get into the more advanced levels of mindfulness practice. So it's important, at least at first, to focus on developing concentration. Once your concentration improves you'll be able to put more focus into exercising mindfulness. You'll start noticing why your mind strays (was it a thought or feeling? What was the thought?), as opposed to simply noticing your mind stray and refocusing on your object of meditation.

2. Pick simple objects

In the beginning you're going to want to pick an easy object of meditation. Then, once your skill improves, you can pick more difficult objects. At first, I'd suggest practicing mindful breathing for a couple of weeks. Whether you're at your desk, at a stoplight, in between places, or sitting down for an extended meditation session. Just stop what you're doing and follow your breath with mindfulness. Focus your concentration on each exhale and inhale and let your mind quiet. If your mind seems a bit chaotic, don't worry. This is perfectly normal and might last a few weeks before really beginning to calm down. Refer back to the chapters "Mindful Breathing" and "Mindful Sitting" for detailed instructions on how to practice mindful breathing as sitting meditation and as a practice which can be done throughout your day. After a few weeks you can move on to mindful walking, eating, and many other nourishing practices. But continue to practice formal sitting meditation in the morning and/ or night and mindful breathing throughout your day. These are great beginner practices and they'll remain cornerstones of your mindfulness practice even as your skill improves. The reason these are great beginner practices is because they don't require a high level of skill. Walking meditation (or mindful walking) is an example of moving meditation, but it's typically done in a slow manner to where it's easy for a beginner to do. I'd still suggest sticking to mindful breathing for at least the first few weeks though before trying to practice walking meditation at all. Don't rush the process of developing mindfulness. You'll gain nothing from doing so and only end up hurting your practice.

3. Pick moving objects

Know that it's best, at first, to pick objects of mindfulness which involve movement. The reason for this is that it's much easier to keep your concentration on something which is constantly changing and moving. The fundamental practices are great because they provide this: breath goes in and out constantly and your steps are well...steps. You can absolutely practice mindfulness of, say, your body while lying down. Simple mindfulness of the body is a very relaxing practice which can help improve the quality of your sleep. But if you're sitting perfectly still then you'll have a hard time in the beginning keeping your concentration. This is just in the beginning though. Once you improve your concentration you'll be able to practice mindfulness of anything with relative ease.

3. Sit often

Sitting meditation really is the cornerstone of all meditative practice. It was my first experience with mindfulness and I'd suggest it be your first experience with meditation of any kind. Adopting a daily practice of sitting meditation is very important. If you try to start practicing mindfulness without making sitting meditation a part of your daily practice then it will be much more difficult to get to a point where your mind becomes quiet. And later, sitting meditation will aid in your efforts to obtain a clear mind. No matter how far a Zen monk goes in their practice, they always sit and often two to three times a day. Remember to think of sitting meditation as your practice time to keep you sharp. Every great athlete practices the fundamentals of their craft on a daily basis. No matter how good they become, they practice the fundamentals. For spiritual practice, one of these fundamentals is sitting meditation.

4. Schedule mindfulness

As I'll talk about in the next chapter, part of why it's difficult to establish mindfulness as a daily practice is that it's something you do throughout your day as opposed to something you usually plan for or schedule. This is great for obvious reasons, but it also means that in the beginning of your practice you can go entire days and just altogether forget to be mindful of anything. Because of this fact it's important to actually schedule part of your practice, at least at first. This will help you develop your mindfulness, increase the chance of you remembering to be mindful during the rest of your day, and give you a clear marker as to how well you're sticking to your practice. If you missed your sitting meditation session, you know you missed. This will help quite a bit at first, trust me. And it's not a bad idea to continue to schedule mindful time, even if it's just your time for sitting meditation.

5. Go easy on yourself

Earlier I talked about the nonjudgmental aspect of mindfulness. Mindfulness is an open acceptance of everything, so those thoughts, feelings, and sensations that keep popping into your mind shouldn't be labelled a bad thing. In fact, they aren't a good thing or a bad thing. Remember, mindfulness is just an observer. You shouldn't be passing judgment, good or bad, on anything including disruptions to your concentration. These distractions are normal. They'll subside for the most part naturally, your mind will quiet over time, and it will bring you a great sense of peace. So don't worry about that. You'll know your practice is really successful not when these distractions subside *but when you start becoming mindful of these distractions.* No matter how many of them you have. Don't get frustrated if at first you can't hold your concentration for more than a few seconds. This is perfectly normal. If you get frustrated just acknowledge the frustration with mindfulness and let it go. Know that these distractions will subside with practice and that your goal is primarily to develop your mindfulness. When you develop the ability to shine the light of mindfulness on these distractions is when the real healing can begin. These disruptions are the things distorting your perception and keeping you from reality as it is, filled with peace, joy, and freedom. No matter what, just keep practicing. With time you'll see the fruits of your labor.

6. Prioritize mindfulness

You won't get far in your practice of mindfulness if you don't prioritize it. This goes for anything in life. This is because right from the beginning you'll be clashing with old habits. Remember last chapter when we talked about our habit energy? Keep in mind that our actions contain a certain amount of energy. That is, that the more often we do something the more energy or "pull" it has. This is our habit energy. We all have this habit energy. What differs from one person to another is where we place this energy.

When you begin practicing mindfulness you'll naturally be "pulled" in other directions constantly. This is your old habit energy attempting to pull you back to your old ways. You can use the other tips and tricks in this chapter, such as making sure to enjoy the process and to pick simple objects of mindfulness, but you'll still need to prioritize your practice. This means, as with establishing any other new habit, you'll have to fight with your old and likely less productive or positive ways. But remember how energy works, the more time and effort you place into something the more pull it will have. Stick with it and gradually it will become easier until the point in which it will take almost no effort at all. And the great thing about mindfulness is that you can do it while doing just about anything. So it's not so much choosing mindfulness over other things, it's more of remembering to be mindful. At first though remember to keep it simple and choose easy objects of mindfulness.

7. Slow it down

We're taught to move quickly, multitask, and ultimately be as productive as possible. This mentality is ingrained in us. It probably started during the industrial revolution, where we as a species became obsessed with speed and productivity. It was all about who could grow the fastest and claim the most land. It was inevitable based on our development as a species, but this mindset has stayed with us to the present day and it's completely against our true nature. We're so used to rushing around all day that a lot of times we never even realize there's another way to live. We think that it's "just how life is". But it's not. And of course, part of the point of mindfulness and meditation is to calm the mind. But this job can and should be handled on both sides. While developing your practice of mindfulness you should also work to become aware of when you're rushing around and when you're not. And aside from helping to calm your mind, if you actively work on slowing down you'll also find more opportunities to practice mindfulness. Because of this it's highly beneficial to analyze your daily schedule. You'll find that opportunities to practice mindfulness are numerous in our daily lives. Walking from point A to point B, sitting in a waiting room, driving to and from work, and just stopping for a moment to follow your breath anywhere and at any time. Slow it down and really start taking the time to enjoy the little moments with mindfulness. It won't take nearly any extra time and very little effort.

8. Be patient

Mindfulness takes time and patience to develop. At first, it will be subtle. Unicorns won't start flying through the air and celebration banners won't drop from the sky. You'll just feel... .a little more alive. A little more present. That's the best way I can describe it. But with practice you'll notice your ability improve. You'll feel more present, more alive, and better able to notice things with your mindfulness. Of course, you'll need to have some indicator that you're practicing correctly. I covered a few great tips so far, but another good one would be to simply practice mindful breathing and sitting meditation often. These are the easiest ways to practice mindfulness and the method of counting your breath, which you'll do during both of those exercises, is the easiest way to tell when you lose your mindfulness and a great way to tell if you're practicing correctly. Remember, mindfulness works like a muscle. The more you work it out, the stronger it gets. Work patiently towards making mindfulness a way of life and you'll develop it into a powerful force for peace and happiness in your life.

9. Let go

When you begin practicing mindfulness you'll probably find it extraordinarily difficult not to become distracted. We covered this earlier, so it shouldn't be of any surprise. But something else will likely happen. You'll have a hard time *convincing your-self* to let go of these distractions. Why is that? Well, we tend to blow everything in our mind out of proportion. What that means is when we have a project due at school, a presentation at work, a big event with the family, or some personal business, we tend to mull over the thing in our heads repeatedly. "Did I remember to do that?" "Did I have them add that?" "What am I going to do about that?" "How is that going to work?" It's an endless cycle of questions and answers. When you begin your mindfulness practice you might have a very hard time convincing yourself to let go of these thoughts for even 10 minutes to sit down and meditate. But it's so important. You might think that you need to keep these things cycling through your brain constantly, otherwise you'll screw something up or just not do as good a job as you could or should, but that's not the case. You only minimize your effectiveness in any given task by hounding over it and never giving your mind any rest. You'd be surprised how refreshed and sharp your mind will be if you allow yourself to step away from something for even a single session of mindful breathing or walking meditation. So learn how to let go of these things and just follow your breath. Let go of everything. The more you practice the easier it will be to do this and the better you'll feel.

10. Have fun

You've probably heard this one a million times before about a million other things, but that's because it's true. It's not just true, it's one of the most important points on this list. Why? Because when we enjoy something our drive to do that thing increases tenfold. Luckily, for the most part, this will come naturally when practicing mindfulness. By the very act of practicing mindfulness your monkey mind will begin to settle and you'll feel an extraordinary sense of tranquility. When I first started practicing mindfulness I felt an amazing sense of peace that seemed to extend throughout the rest of my day. It was rough at first, I can't say that it wasn't difficult. Your mind will likely be bouncing around uncontrollably for the first a couple of weeks, you'll be pretty fidgety, and if you use a timer during sitting meditation you'll find thoughts like "I wonder how much longer I have to go?" popping up regularly. But even so, you'll find yourself feeling great after finishing a session, even if it was just a few minutes long. During this time you really just have to push through the difficulty. But I don't mean literally push or be forceful. Just be mindful of whatever it is you're being mindful of, in the beginning this will be mostly your breath, and as thoughts arise gently acknowledge them and bring your concentration back to your breath. This tough period won't last long at all and during it you'll still get a lot of joy from practicing. Really take time to notice how mindfulness is improving your mood and behavior. If you take time to do this you'll deepen your appreciation of your practice further and find even more drive to continue practicing.

But the real joy is in once your mind has begun to settle and you can just sit. When you can sit, stop, or walk and be mindful without feeling like you want to get up or like you have something you need to get to, you'll know you've reached a real milestone. I can't describe this feeling to you. You just have to feel it for yourself. It's one of the most beautiful and peaceful feelings you'll ever feel in your life. In those moments everything is perfect just as it is and you feel like you could sit forever.

11. Just sit

At first, you might find yourself counting the minutes waiting for your meditation session to be over. This is the wrong mentality. I used to sit down and eventually grow twitchy and fidgety when I knew my session was almost over. If this is happening to you, try not setting a timer for a while. Just sit. If you're too conditioned to "get results" in everything you do then a timer during mindful sitting can be counterproductive at first because all you'll want to do is think "check! That's off my list..." but there's no benefit in that and meditation doesn't work that way. Just sit. After a while this feeling will disappear and instead you'll notice yourself feeling like you could sit forever. And it will feel wonderful.

Tools of Mindfulness

Shortly after beginning my own mindfulness practice something became glaringly obvious to me: it's really easy to forget to be mindful. And I don't mean for a few minutes, I mean for entire days. Especially if you have a typically busy schedule. This is because one of our most common habit energies is the very semi-conscious state I described earlier in the book. We're so conditioned to live in this semi-conscious state that in the beginning we need to remind ourselves to be mindful constantly in order to establish it as a daily practice. Sure, mindfulness is awesome because you can do it *while* doing anything else you typically do in your daily life. But that's part of the very reason why you need tools to help you establish mindfulness as a daily practice. While you might strive to be mindful whenever walking, without things supporting your practice you'll more than likely just forget and walk wherever you go like you always do. That is, semi-conscious, with a mind dispersed between many thoughts and sensations.

In the last chapter, under item number four titled "Schedule mindfulness", I mentioned how scheduling a specific time frame to be mindful, whether you practice mindful sitting, walking, or something else, helps support and establish your practice. But this only aids in the process. It will still be easy to forget to practice while going about your day. Towards that end, tangible tools like symbols and reminders are something I've made great use of in establishing my own mindfulness practice. Tools of mindfulness are tools which interact with one of the six sense organs: touch, taste, sight, smell, sound, and mind. In Buddhism, mind is considered a "sense organ". I think it helps personal and spiritual development greatly to interpret mind as an organ which receives sensations much the same way as our other traditional sense organs do. Here, I'm talking particularly about either a sound to remind you, a sight to instill feelings in you, an idea to conjure a state of mind in you, or a combination.

In this chapter we'll talk about how to set up reminders (both audio and visual) which naturally help you develop the habit of mindfulness, how to utilize objects as constant objects of mindfulness during your day, and how to create a pocket-sized resource to not only help remind you to practice mindfulness but which also gives you a way to trigger mindfulness during all of your regular daily activities. Again, these are all techniques I myself have used personally and which have helped me develop the practice of mindfulness in my own life. I hope some of these can be of use to you. They were of great use to me!

Symbols of Mindfulness

Symbols can be powerful forms of reinforcement and support. A necklace, a ring, a bracelet, something you keep in your pocket like a rock, or anything else you might think of. It's about creating your own symbol for mindfulness and awakening which you carry on you at all times. It reminds you to be mindful, and it also acts as a sort of refuge. When you touch your symbol of mindfulness, you can enter a state of mindfulness. No matter where you are, no matter what you're doing, your symbol of mindfulness is a great way to bring yourself back to reality and calm your mind and body.

A while back I purchased a small gold lotus pendant, which I still wear to this day. I thought it might be helpful in reminding me to be mindful and of the importance of my spiritual practice as a whole. I decided on the lotus flower because it symbolizes awakening, so it reminds me of my practice and the overall purpose. A symbol which you keep on you throughout your day really is a great way to remind yourself to be mindful. This one thing helped my practice greatly. I personally wasn't used to wearing jewelry of any kind, so if you're like me you'll have to try different things out to see what you prefer. You can also carry something like a small and smooth flat rock. It will fit in your pocket or purse but at the same time be just bulky enough to remind you that it's there from time to time throughout your day.

Whatever symbol you decide on, if you decide to use one then use it wisely. Take it seriously, remember why you're wearing or carrying this symbol. Don't let it just become something you carry which you pass over. Remember, if you're passing over it then you're passing over your practice.

The Bell of Mindfulness

Remember the chapter on mindful breathing? Practicing mindful breathing throughout your day can itself be a great way to develop mindfulness further. By setting reminders on your phone (or tablet, if you carry it on you) or posting a reminder on the wall of a room you step into every day such as your restroom at home or office at work, you can help develop mindfulness as a daily practice. One of the most effective ways I've found of developing mindfulness as a daily practice is by setting up simple alarm reminders on your phone. I'd suggest setting them for the same timeframe I mentioned in the *Mindful Breathing* chapter. Set the alarm to go off every hour and plan to practice mindful breathing for about one minute once the alarm goes off.

I like to use a bell sound set as my alarm sound. Many Buddhist temples have bells, very similar to church bells, which they sound when a session of meditation begins and ends. Every time the bell goes off I imagine the bell sounding at one of these temples and, no matter where I am, transport myself to a place of peace and quiet. When this bell sounds everything stops. I don't listen to the excuses I try to give myself about "oh, let me just finish this one thing", or "I'll get to that in just a minute". I stop everything and just breathe mindfully. No matter where I am I stop. If I'm not comfortable I immediately go somewhere that I am. Just breathe. Let this be your daily vacation time. No matter where you are, for one minute every hour you're transported to a place of pure peace and tranquility. When you come back you'll feel refreshed and ready to tackle anything. And not only that. By doing this one practice you'll be reminded to be mindful throughout the rest of your day.

This one practice was a huge help in developing my daily practice. Not only are you reminding yourself to practice mindful breathing every hour, but because you're practicing mindfulness every hour of every day (I typically have them set to start going off around 8AM since my kids are awake by then, wouldn't want to wake them early...) you gradually begin to remember to practice mindfulness while doing other things throughout your day so it supports the development of your entire practice. But as with all of the tools discussed in this chapter, you need to take it seriously. You might find yourself, for a time, disregarding this alarm. If you find yourself doing this you need to remind yourself why your practice is important, dust yourself off, and just get back on the wagon. It's natural to run into some bumps along the way. So remember, go easy on yourself and just keep chugging along.

Towards that same end you can also post physical signs that you type or handwrite and place them on the wall of rooms you walk into every day such as your restroom, kitchen, office, and even your car. You can write or draw whatever you want on it as long as it reminds you to be mindful during your daily life. For instance, you could have a poster or sign that symbolizes walking meditation in your bedroom that sits on the back of your bedroom door. This way, each time you walk out of your bedroom in the morning you're reminded to walk mindfully. If you tend to rush around at the office and build up most of your stress and anxiety there you can place one on the back of your office door or laminate and place a small one on the surface of your desk. Signs work great. The only thing about them is that if you don't take them seriously from the start it becomes easy to ignore or simply pass over them. Whichever one of these tools you use, you must take them and your overall practice seriously. As I mentioned in the last paragraph, if this is a problem then remind yourself why your practice is important and get back on track. In this case you could always add these reasons to the very sign that reminds you to be mindful. That way, you're simultaneously reminded to practice mindfulness as well as why it's so important to do so in the first place. There's a lot of options for making use of reminders. Do whatever works for you.

The Pocket Book of Mindfulness

When Zen master Thich Nhat Hanh first began his monastic life as a Buddhist monk he was given a small book. The book, "The Essential Discipline for Daily Use", was written by the Zen master Doc The (pronounced "tay") and given to novice monks in order to help them develop the practice of mindfulness. The book, as Nhat Hanh describes it, was no more than 40 pages long from front to back and was made up of short verses which they would recite to themselves while doing specific tasks in order to awaken their minds (i.e. practice mindfulness). The book included verses for each specific activity that a monk or nun might do throughout his or her day. Such as waking up:

Just awakened, I hope that every person will attain great awareness and see in complete clarity.

And washing their hands...

Washing my hands, I hope that every person will have pure hands to receive reality.

Thich Nhat Hanh has since expanded on that original idea by adding a few modern meditations of his own such as a telephone meditation and a meditation for riding a bike. The telephone meditation is four lines. You breathe in when reading the first line (silently to yourself), out for the second line, in for the third, and out once more for the fourth:

Words can travel thousands of kilometers.

They can build more understanding and love.

I vow that what I'm going to say is going to promote mutual understanding and love.

And every word I say will be beautiful like flowers.

As you can see, the first two mentioned were one-liners and the third was a full verse. There's no set way to do this, the point is that they're words to help you practice mindfulness and conjure a state of mindfulness and greater awakening. Overall, I loved the idea of the book and thought it would be an incredible tool to help myself **develop the practice of mindfulness**. So I decided to make my own "Essential Discipline".

Long-term happiness doesn't just fall into your lap. Unless you make the decision to prioritize something, you've got nothing more than a shot in the dark at accomplishing it. But how do you do this with an already busy schedule? Trust me, I know how you feel. I, at the time of writing this, have a nine month old and a three year-old. Just they by themselves are a handful like no other let alone my other responsibilities. But this can be helped by a number of things. We just have to get creative. This is why I liked the idea of "The Essential Discipline for Daily Use" so much. I thought, what if I created my own version of the Zen master's book in order to help me adopt the practice of mindfulness in my everyday life? That was the birth of the pocket book of mindfulness.

Adopting the practice of mindfulness isn't easy, no matter who you are. But this book is the perfect companion for the modern-day man or woman to cultivate the practice of mindfulness whether you lead a busy family life or fast-paced corporate life (and anywhere in between). I liked the idea of having a book which outlined all the various moments throughout the day where one could practice mindfulness and realized that if I did it old school – that is if I literally bought a physical (handheld) notebook and kept it on me at all times- it would be a great way to remind myself to practice mindfulness as well. Feeling it in your pocket, you're constantly reminded that it's there. Well, turns out, it worked. As soon as I started using it I was not only constantly reminded to practice mindfulness, I knew how to put myself into a state of mindfulness no matter what I was doing.

And then I began associating a sense of peace and happiness with the act of taking the book out, which encouraged me to use it to practice mindfulness even more often. Which brings me to the many reasons why the pocket book of mindfulness is a great tool for helping one develop mindfulness.

First, it constantly reminds you to practice mindfulness. It's simple- it's a physical book that you handwrite and keep in your pocket or wallet. It's physically obstructive, or at least noticeable enough that you're constantly reminded to practice mindfulness throughout your day when you sit down or reach for your wallet. What's great too is, after a while of reading and practicing each phrase you'll start to automatically remember to practice and recite the applicable phrase to yourself without even needing the book any longer.

It's also great because it shows you how to practice mindfulness no matter what you're doing: This is the original purpose of the book. Within it exists various short verses, as we discussed earlier, to help you develop your practice of mindfulness. No matter what you're doing the book has a phrase which you can use to take control of your consciousness and enter mindfulness. If you think you'll be taking the book out more often than you're comfortable with at first, don't worry. After a while you'll memorize certain phrases and won't have to take the book out nearly as often.

Lastly, it provides positive reinforcement for your practice. You'll notice that, after a while of using the book, the book itself becomes a symbol of the benefits of your practice. Inner peace, happiness and clarity all become associated with opening your book and reading a verse. This is a great source of reinforcement for your practice. Which, as we talked about earlier, is necessary given how easy it is to forget why we're practicing. If you're constantly reminded of the benefits and beauty of your practice you'll not only continue to practice but your practice will strengthen.

Building Your Own Book of Mindfulness

In order to create your own book of mindfulness you'll just need: a small pocket-sized notebook, a pen, and a little inspiration. For the pocket-sized notebook I'd suggest Moleskine. That's what I made my book with and it's served me perfectly. You can get them at Barnes & Noble if you have one around you, otherwise you can find them easily online. Feel free to use whatever makes you comfortable though, there's absolutely no guidelines to this. You're simply writing verses on paper in a format that allows you to keep it in a noticeable place throughout your day.

Next, you'll need a pen. Nothing special here, right? But I would like to mention two important points which I learned in making my own book. First, try to use a pen that doesn't bleed too much. And second, make sure after writing something to keep the book open for a bit in order to let the ink dry. This isn't a big deal, but as you can see from the images below the ink will really spread unless you do this because of how many times you open and close the book.

And lastly, you can take the verses I have listed below as-is as well as examples for creating verses that apply more specifically to your own life. I listed three examples earlier but below are a few more entries I have in my own book of mindfulness including some verses I created for modern life (driving, the internet).

Home

The first page of my book of mindfulness is about the practice of "going home" or returning to yourself. We all lose ourselves in struggles and challenges from time to time, but by practicing mindfulness we can go back to ourselves and regain inner peace and clarity.

Present moment

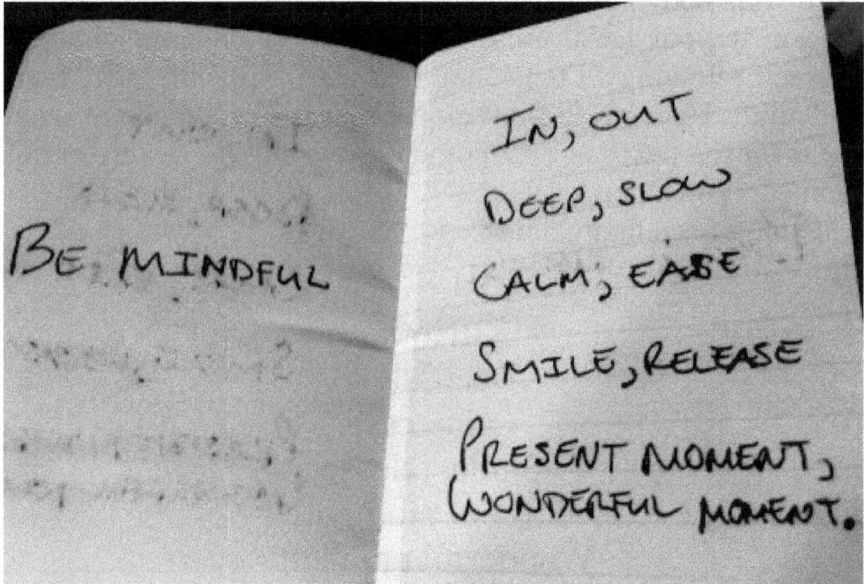

Present moment, wonderful moment is a poem written by Thich Nhat Hanh. I really liked it and thought it would be the perfect verse for stopping and following my breath (when feeling stressed, overwhelmed or needing to calm down for whatever other reason) so I decided to put it at the beginning of the book . I've since used it more than any other verse in the book. Reading it brings me a great sense of inner peace. Each word in the poem up to "release" refers to what you're supposed to do as you breathe in or out. I typically breathe in and out 2-3 times for each line to enhance the practice. Breathe in on the first word of each line and breathe out for the second. Breathe in on "Present moment" and breathe out on "Wonderful moment".

So as you read "deep", make sure you take a deep breath. As

you read "slow" make sure you take a slow breath. As you go adopt each new word into your practice. First deep breathing, then slow deep breathing, then as you breathe slowly and deeply calm your body and ease your mind, half-smile to release the tension in your facial muscles and then on "release" imagine yourself releasing all tension and stress from your entire body and mind. Then on "Present moment, wonderful moment" simply savor the peace of this moment. Relish in the beauty of this moment. You'll never get it back. This is a very calming practice which I've used many times.

In, out
Deep, slow
Calm, ease
Smile, release
Present moment,
Wonderful moment.

Dealing with anger

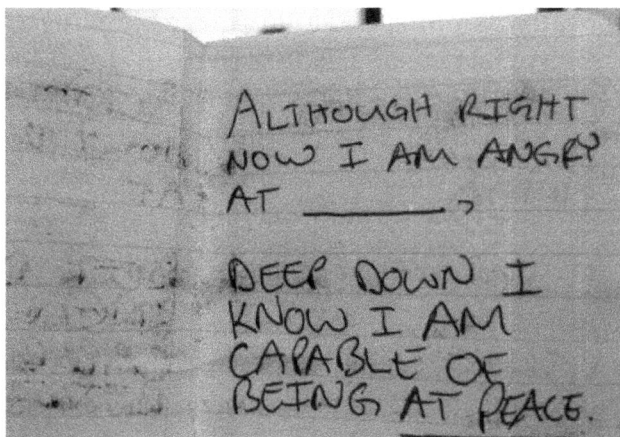

This is another verse which I adapted from Thich Nhat Hanh's work as I thought it would be highly useful given the "toolbox" nature of the Book of Mindfulness. I thought, why does the book only have to help with becoming mindful during specific activities? This verse helps you regain hold of your consciousness when anger takes over, no matter what you're doing. Breathe in and out for the first line and in and out again for the second line. After reading the line below you can continue to breathe mindfully until the emotion calms.

Although right now I am angry at _____ ,

Deep down I know I am capable of being at peace.

Driving meditation

As I place my hands on this wheel I enter a state of mindfulness.

I know I am sitting here, driving this car.

I vow to treat other drivers with patience and compassion.

And I will renew my sense of inner peace with each turn of the wheel.

Internet meditation

As I place my hands on this device I enter a state of mindfulness.

My breath is my companion to the connected world.

I know where I am, what I'm doing and why I'm doing it.

And I vow to consume only those things which nurture my mind.

Working meditation

As I enter this building I also enter a state of mindfulness.

I will treat all tasks with the same level of importance I place on taking care of my boys. (You can fill in the blank here, this is my own)

My breath will guide all important decisions.

I vow to treat others with compassion and will use deep listening when speaking with teammates.

This is only a sliver of what you can include in your own book. If you really put the work in to utilize the pocket book of mindfulness it can be a valuable tool to advance your practice.

Start Your Adventure

My intention with *The Little Book of Mindfulness* was to provide a resource which broke mindfulness down from A to Z and gave the reader everything they needed to make mindfulness a part of their lives. I *hope The Little Book of Mindfulness* has done just that for you.

In Part 1, we discussed the origins of mindfulness, what mindfulness is, what it isn't, and the benefits or reasons to practice mindfulness. In Part 2, we covered practicing mindfulness through the fundamental activities of mindful sitting, mindful walking, and mindful breathing. We also discussed how to practice mindful eating, cleaning, working in mindfulness, and how to be fully present with mindfulness for experiences with friends and family. And in Part 3, we discussed how to actually make mindfulness a daily practice, or habit. We discussed my best intangible tips and tricks for developing mindfulness as a way of life such as to have fun with it, prioritize your practice, and tips for specific practices, as well as an entire chapter on tangible tools for developing mindfulness such as reminders, symbols, and the pocket book of mindfulness.

But no matter how much value this book has provided for you, it won't amount to anything unless you take action. You can read ten, twenty, even thirty books on mindfulness or anything else in life for that matter. But if you don't then get up and *apply* that knowledge, nothing will change. You'll stay in the same position you're in now with the same level of happiness and fulfillment. Now's the time to take the information within this book and apply it to create positive change in your life. Learn about mindfulness, understand its importance, and then apply both the practices themselves and the tips and tricks to establishing mindfulness as a daily practice that I described in this section.

Take time to practice sitting meditation every day, go for a short mindful walk after work, and breathe mindfully throughout your day. Sit and eat in mindfulness while being fully present for each bite. Be completely present when spending time with family and friends, appreciating their presence and feeling their love. Learn to live deeply and treat every typically mundane activity with reverence and complete attention so as to train yourself to find peace and happiness in the simplest of things by touching the very ground of your being. And open *yourself* up to the light of mindfulness. Let all of your insecurities, deep-seated emotions, and conditions rise to the surface so that you can allow the mind and body's natural healing process to take place.

Mindfulness is meant to be *lived*, not studied. It's about living deeply and seeing into the true nature of yourself and the world around you. So get out there, start really living, and never look back. Shine the light of mindfulness on your entire life. Wherever you go, *be there*. Whatever you do, *do it with you entire being*. Transform your life one moment at a time. This is your life and *it's now or never*. Let mindfulness guide you to a happier, more peaceful, and more harmonious existence. Your adventure starts today.

Peace,
Matt

P.S. Developing mindfulness as a way of life isn't easy, but it's infinitely rewarding. If you need help along the way I'd be more than willing in any way that I can. My home online is my blog Buddhaimonia (buddhaimonia.com). I write new articles weekly and would love to see you stop by sometime. Continued reading and teaching is healthy for any self-development practice and I aim to provide the best content possible towards that purpose. Feel free to leave a comment on an article, message me on Twitter or Google+, or send me an email and I'll do everything I can to help.

The 9 Most Frequently Asked Questions on Mindfulness and Meditation

FAQ 1: What's the difference between mindfulness and meditation?

At this point you might be wondering: what exactly is the difference between mindfulness and meditation? **Mindfulness is itself a form of meditation.** One of various forms of meditation. Which is why, as you might have noticed, the word meditation has been used in place of, or alongside, mindfulness at various points in the book thus far. There's just certain more traditional ways of referring to different types of mindfulness practices which can often make things confusing for a beginner.

Mindful sitting is traditionally called sitting meditation, simply meditation, or more recently mindfulness meditation. Mindful walking is traditionally called walking meditation, not mindful walking. Things like this can make it confusing for someone just starting out, especially someone who's learning on their own without the guidance of a formal teacher, which is common in the age of the internet.

So, if mindfulness is a form of meditation, what exactly is meditation? Meditation covers a pretty broad spectrum of techniques. But there is a central theme. All meditation has to do with developing the mind. In a nutshell, meditation is **a mental technique used to develop or maintain the mind.** Like mindfulness, meditation can be defined in a number of ways. What's important is just that you get the general idea. Your true understanding of meditation will come when you actually begin to meditate.

FAQ 2: How exactly is slowing down and taking time to do something completely unrelated to my work supposed to make me more productive?

While productivity isn't the point of mindfulness or life in general, and before anything this should be realized, as I mentioned earlier in the chapter there's nothing necessarily wrong with wanting to be more productive. You just need to understand that there are times and ways that productivity is helpful (positive productivity) and other times and ways where it's harmful (negative productivity). If you figure out how you can get your work done in a third of the time that it used to take you and that allows you to get home to your kids faster each day, that's *positive productivity*. If you decide to start taking your work home and instead of playing with your son you work at the kitchen table all night while your son sits and plays by himself, this is *negative productivity*.

Another example would be that if you decided to stop taking your lunch break in order to get an extra half-hour or hour of work in each day, and consequently never even slightly rest your mind during your average work day, this would be negative productivity because it will actually hinder your performance more than that half-hour or hour of extra work could ever make up for. But worst of all, by doing so you hurt your overall mental well-being. On the other hand, if you were to decide to take part of your half-hour or hour lunch each day and practice mindful sitting for 15-20 minutes, this would be positive productivity. By doing so you'd be giving your mind the best rest it could get in the middle of a work day by completely taking your mind away from work for an extended period of time. This will greatly improve your performance. But best of all, it increases your overall mental well-being.

Positive productivity improves the well-being of yourself and those around you. This can include things that don't have anything to do with your work but instead make you more efficient. By taking a break to do something which will make you sharper, more alert, more optimistic, and/or more energetic you increase your effectiveness, and therefore productivity, in any given task tenfold. Negative productivity harms the well-being of yourself and those around you. Negative productivity often just makes us *feel* more productive and either doesn't make us more productive at all or actually hurts our productivity. If you use these as your guiding principles towards productivity you're sure to become maximally productive while simultaneously improving instead of harming your well-being.

I completely understand the productivity junkie mentality because I was that guy too. I didn't understand the point of doing something completely unrelated to my work or how that could actually make me more productive. I was the epitome of a productivity junkie. Everything I did that I felt wasn't naturally productive towards my work I tried to do at the same time as something that was. When I did work I tried to be as quick as possible and was constantly looking for ways to squeeze more time out of each day to get more work done. It turns out none of those things make you all that more productive. In fact, they can make you far less productive. But when you allow your mind to step away for a period of time from something that's been sitting in your mind and truly rest, you'll notice yourself as being far more creative, effective, and therefore productive when coming back to it. It's just the way the mind works, there's nothing more to it. We need rest. It's completely unhealthy for us to stay on any task for an extended period of time with no rest. A great guiding principle would be to use your mindfulness itself to keep tabs on the condition of your mind while working. If you're trying out things that can make you more productive, but feel your mind becoming stressed as a result of these things, it's probably a good idea to stop doing them.

FAQ 3: How long can I expect to practice before seeing results?

I wouldn't bother worrying about when you're going to see results or not. You shouldn't be so focused on "getting results" when it comes to your spiritual practice or even just mindfulness in itself. Of course, it would be wrong to say that you started your practice for no reason. That just doesn't make any sense. You started wanting something, and this could be called a result. But what I really mean by that is you should be more focused on the practice itself. Know why you began your mindfulness practice, find confirmation of your practice in that and then let go of it. Practice without any expectations. Only once you let go will you obtain the greatest "results". If you keep hanging onto ideas of "I do this because I want to get this in return" then you'll never find true peace.

"OK, but just like you said I'm still going into this because I'm interested in gaining something", you say. I'm sure you, like most others including myself, began or want to begin practicing mindfulness in order to calm your mind and feel more peaceful and happy. If that's the case then you'll feel concrete effects of your practice almost immediately. When I say you can find true peace and happiness *in this moment*, I mean it. Of course, you'll need to develop your ability to experience the greatest results.

In all likelihood your first couple of weeks will be tough. You'll experience your monkey mind at its greatest intensity. Ultimately it all depends on how quiet (or loud) your mind is going into practice. Either way, don't judge yourself. It doesn't matter how quiet or loud your mind is, just that you practice diligently. For the most part, the "rewards" exist in the very moment of practicing and not in some far-off goal. This is an important lesson to learn. With mindfulness you'll learn to appreciate the present moment as it is in all its beauty

For me in my own practice, in the beginning seeing my mind gradually quiet and feeling the increasing sense of peace within myself as my practice developed was more than enough confirmation and encouragement for me to keep practicing. That started happening after just a few weeks and was rather significant.

FAQ 4: Can't I just sit down however I want when I meditate? Do I have to sit in the full-lotus in order to get the greatest benefit from sitting meditation?

No, you don't have to sit in any particular position. The purpose of the full lotus is simply that it's the most stable sitting position available to us. When you sit in the full lotus while being supported by a proper cushion you'll see what I mean. In the full lotus you feel extremely stable. Even more stable than sitting in a chair.

You can meditate in whatever sitting position you'd like. But be careful, a stable sitting position and proper posture are very important in a regular meditation practice. The full lotus is the most stable position by far and, once you get used to it, a very comfortable position to meditate in. Because of the stability of the full lotus it also removes potential bodily distractions from sitting meditation. You're free to let your mind and body vanish and simply sit with your breath.

You should strive to eventually sit in the full lotus. This is a difficult position to sit in even with practice for some which is why I mentioned earlier in the chapter that you can sit in the half lotus or even sit cross-legged or on a chair if neither of those are comfortable for you. In no way is any specific sitting position a requirement. Don't let anyone tell you so. Sit in whatever position you can and meditate diligently.

FAQ 5: The same thought keeps coming into my mind while meditating, what does it mean?

Don't worry, this is normal. Because everything is an object of your consciousness, mindfulness is really about becoming fully aware of your own complete body and mind. Your thoughts and emotions being a part of that. If the same thought keeps creeping into your mind during meditation, then, as you do with any thought, simply acknowledge it each time it comes to the surface and then bring your focus back to your breath. Do this as many times as necessary. You're letting the emotion run its course. Whether it's a specific fear, anger, or some limiting belief, this is a good thing because it's a clear sign that your mindfulness is improving.

If you stick to your practice you will slowly and gently unfold your mind, watching all your fear, anger and stress dissipate. This is why it's important to practice mindfulness in your everyday life. Even if you meditate every single day it won't be enough. You need to work on being mindful during your everyday life in order to uncover all the various afflictions blocking you from experiencing the ultimate level of peace and happiness.

FAQ 6: Everywhere I read I'm being told to acknowledge the thought and then "let it go". What does that even mean?

What's important is that you acknowledge the thought with mindfulness. By acknowledging the thought with mindfulness that in itself is a nonjudgmental action. You aren't judging the thought or yourself for having the thought. By "let it go" the teacher is probably often referring to the nonjudgmental aspect of mindfulness, whether they realize it or not. It's not a bad description, I like it myself because it reminds one of the nonjudgmental aspect of mindfulness, but more detail needs to be given of the action instead of just "let it go".

The only action that will precede acknowledging the thought with mindfulness will be you bringing your concentration back to the object of mindfulness, be it your breath, steps, broom, dishes, food, or whatever you're being mindful of. Essentially, because mindfulness is itself by nature nonjudgmental, there will be no letting go. There will simply be no clinging. Mindfulness is what observes the thought, but mindfulness does not grab hold of anything in the first place. So there is nothing to let go of.

More often than not the same thought will reappear constantly. Instead of trying to kindly get the elephant out the door, only to find him resisting, imagine yourself talking to a giraffe and the elephant just walks up and interrupts you. Bringing your concentration back to your object of mindfulness isn't letting the thought go, it's simply turning away from the elephant and continuing your conversation with the giraffe. Yes, the elephant will continue to try and interrupt. But simply being with these interruptions in order to heal them is the very nature of meditative practice. It will take some time to heal. Just keep sitting and be with the elephant. Don't make him leave, just sit with him and eventually he'll calm down and stop interrupting you. When this happens, the thought or emotion (the elephant) will have subsided.

FAQ 7: How do I know when I'm practicing mindfulness?

At first, you're going to be confused as to whether or not you're really practicing mindfulness. So, you're supposed to read some words on a page and then just....hope you're doing it right? That's where faith comes in. I don't mean faith in a higher power, but I am talking about belief in something. In this case, that means belief in the teaching or instruction of this book. Trust the instruction in this book and just practice. Keep practicing and, with time, you'll get the hang of it.

There are some good ways to identify that you're practicing correctly. The best place to start is with what I mentioned on point 6 in the *Mindfulness is...* chapter, but there are some questions you can ask yourself to further ensure you're practicing correctly. Ask yourself these questions once you've been practicing for a few weeks (the answer to each of these is likely to be yes if you're practicing correctly):

Q1: Do I feel happier and more at peace than I did before I started practicing mindfulness?

Q2: Do I feel less stress and mental exhaustion than before?

Q3: Am I feeling less angry and more patient than I did before?

Q4: While being mindful, am I sensing the interruptions that arise in my mind and body?

Q5: When I become mindful, do I feel like I just turned the light switch on to my life?

Q1-Q3 are clear indicators that you're not only practicing mindfulness but that you're practice is working.

If you answered no to Q4, you might be concentrating too hard. That is, forcing your concentration to the point where you'll give yourself a headache. Softly direct your concentration to the object of mindfulness and softly redirect it when your concentration lapses.

And in regards to Q5, remember that mindfulness is a conscious decision. The moment you decide to become mindful is a conscious decision, and an act, committed by you. You should feel an immediate change in your awareness when making this conscious decision.

FAQ 8: I often go days without remembering to practice mindfulness. I feel like it's just not working for me. What am I supposed to do?

Tackling that very good question is the very purpose of Part 3. This is something you'll undoubtedly encounter when beginning to develop mindfulness as a daily practice. The chapter *Tools of Mindfulness* is about just that- overcoming our natural ability to forget to practice. Most of us are pretty busy. And so it can be really easy to let an entire day go by and forget to practice mindfulness altogether when we're used to rushing around from the time we wake up until the time we lay our heads down to rest. If you use one or more of the techniques I outline in *Tools of Mindfulness* chapter then eventually your practice will grow and you'll be practicing on a daily basis.

You might notice during this time that you begin to slow down. I mean that you begin to move more slowly throughout your day than you did previously. And yet, you'll be getting more done. This is one of the beautiful benefits of mindfulness. Mindfulness will help you realize that all that rushing around never made you more productive. And now you have a better way.

FAQ 9: I can't sit still, how on earth am I supposed to meditate?

All the more reason to sit! Those who have the most difficulty sitting still are the ones who need mindfulness the most. If you're constantly moving to the point where you can't imagine yourself sitting still for more than a few minutes at a time then your mind is very, very busy. And the busier your mind, the more stressed and anxious you are.

If all you do is learn how to stop and follow your breath from time to time you'll completely transform how you feel on a day to day basis. Those with the most difficulty sitting are typically the ones who end up appreciating the practice the most because they derive the most meaning from it. We often have to learn from experience in order to really appreciate something. If you've experienced a chaotic mind then you'll truly appreciate the peace you find from adopting the practice of mindfulness in your daily life.

Thank You

The truth is, we may or may not ever meet one another. We may never speak. The world is a big place and I won't ever know and definitely won't ever be able to meet everyone who reads my work. So it's because of this that I wanted to take a second to say thank you. A big thank you. Even if we never meet again I wanted to let you know how much I appreciate you taking the time to read *The Little Book of Mindfulness*. It means so much to me that you took the time to sit down and read my work. From the bottom of my heart, *thank you*.

I worked harder than I ever have in my life to write *The Little Book of Mindfulness*. Despite being in the middle of moving my family to a new home, raising my two wild boys (who, at the time of writing this, are 9 months and 3 years old), working 40 hours a week, growing and maintaining my blog, and a whole list of other responsibilities, I finished the book and made it out in one piece. But it took a lot from more than just me. I also wanted to thank my wife Edith. She's been the best mommy to our two little dudes and been nothing but supportive of my work from day one. She, before anyone else, told me I should write. I also wanted to thank my mom for always being there. She's been nothing but supportive from day one as well. She and my wife were my first two readers on Buddhaimonia, before anyone else even knew it existed.

A quick note about distributing The Little Book of Mindfulness:

Feel free to distribute this to friends, family, and acquaintances. Just do me a favor and either direct them to buddhaimonia.com so that they can have a chance to sign up to my email list and get their own copy or at least let them know where you got it. I bring out a lot of free content on my blog, but with a family of four that depends on me to put food on the table, and a dream of someday being able to write fulltime, I can't do this completely for free. Your time is precious, so I appreciate that you've decided to spend some of that time with me and *The Little Book of Mindfulness*.

Thank you!

About the Author

Author Matt Valentine

Matt Valentine is the founder of Buddhaimonia (Buddhaimonia.com) and a self-published author. He writes weekly on his blog about personal and spiritual development at large including a range of topics such as mindfulness, meditation, conscious living, self-mastery, relationships, productivity, and simple living. Matt believes that spirituality is simply about learning how to live deeply in the present moment and that by doing so we can discover the greatest gifts that life can offer.

Matt lives with his family in Los Angeles, California. You can learn more about Matt at Buddhaimonia.com/about.

More from Matt Valentine

Zen for Everyday Life

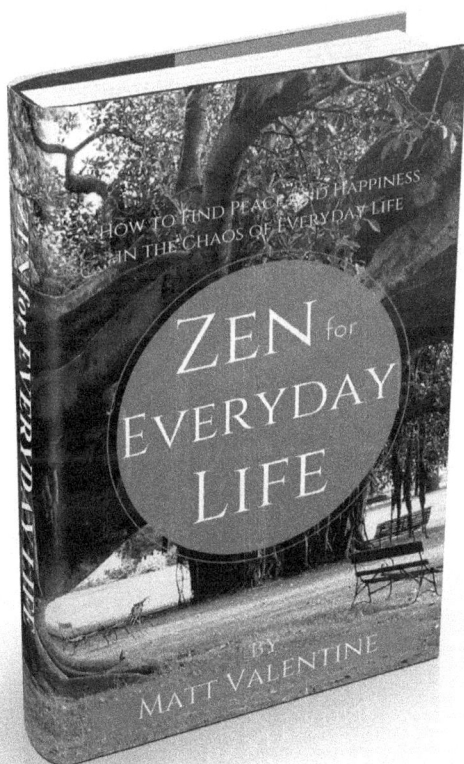

Coming soon (December 2014), *Zen for Everyday Life: How to Find Peace and Happiness in the Chaos of Everyday Life*

will be my next book. Zen for Everyday Life shows you from beginning to end how to develop a daily practice which nourishes your mind and body and helps you and your loved ones discover true peace and happiness. In it, I'll talk about letting go of the common misconceptions we hold onto with regards to finding peace and happiness, discovering the power of making the most of the present moment, using mindfulness to guide your practice, finding peace in everyday activities, making peace when relating with others, nurturing peace by creating an environment which instills harmony with your practice and the rest of your life, maintaining peace despite life getting in the way and throwing you surprises (as it so loves to do), and much more.

Zen for Everyday Life will be available soon, so look for it at buddhaimonia.com and Amazon!

Buddhaimonia.com

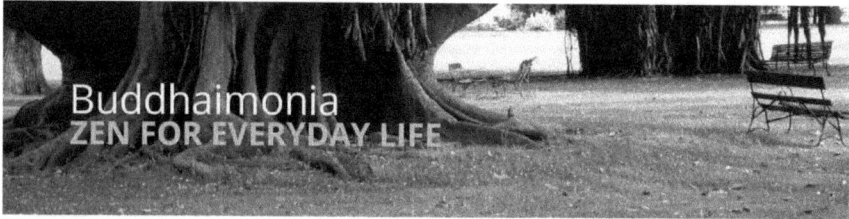

I write weekly on my blog Buddhaimonia (buddhaimonia. com) about spiritual and personal development. The blog's slogan is the same as the title for my second book, *Zen for Everyday Life*. My blog is about taking principles which have existed in spiritual traditions for thousands of years, particularly Zen Buddhism, pairing them with modern knowledge and wisdom and showing the average person how to apply those techniques and strategies in their everyday lives. Ultimately, my blog is designed to help people develop a practice which nourishes their minds and bodies on a daily basis and leads them to true peace and happiness and their greatest potential.

As you might imagine then, my blog includes a pretty broad spectrum of topics. I write on topics such as mindfulness, other various forms of meditation, mindful living (or conscious living, a huge topic in itself), simple living, productivity, overcoming obstacles, dealing with strong emotions, and much more.

My goal is to provide as much insanely useful content as possible. I'd love to see you stop by sometime and check it out. And when you do, let me know what you thought of *The Little Book of Mindfulness*!

www.ingramcontent.com/pod-product-compliance
Lightning Source LLC
Chambersburg PA
CBHW070637030426
42337CB00020B/4051